GREATEST AMERICAN POETS

**COLLECTABLE
EDITION**

CLASSICS

Published 2024

FiNGERPRINT! CLASSiCS
An imprint of Prakash Books India Pvt. Ltd

113/A, Darya Ganj,
New Delhi-110 002
Email: info@prakashbooks.com/sales@prakashbooks.com

Fingerprint Publishing
@FingerprintP
@fingerprintpublishingbooks
www.fingerprintpublishing.com

ISBN: 978 93 5856 638 3

Poetry has long held a unique place in American literature, capturing the essence of the nation's history, culture, and dreams. From the early pioneers who explored the vast landscapes of a growing nation to the modern wordsmiths shaping contemporary thought, American poetry has flourished with an unparalleled richness and diversity.

In *Greatest American Poets*, we embark on an enchanting journey through time, delving deep into the works of the fantastic writers who have crafted poetic masterpieces that have endured for generations. This remarkable compilation features the works of renowned American wordsmiths such as Emily Dickinson, Ralph Waldo Emerson, Henry David Thoreau, Walt Whitman, Henry Wadsworth Longfellow, and many more. This book is a celebration of their contributions to American literary heritage and an exploration of the themes and emotions that resonate with readers across time and place.

Greatest American Poets is a celebration of the power of words, the diversity of voices, and the universality of emotions. It invites readers to immerse themselves in the lyrical beauty and profound insights that have shaped American poetry. Explore the breathtaking range of emotions and the intimate moments captured by these wordsmiths. Their poems have stood the test of time, transcending boundaries and offering solace, inspiration, and profound insights to generations of readers.

CONTENTS

EMILY DICKINSON

WALT WHITMAN

ROBERT FROST

EDGAR ALLAN POE

ANNE BRADSTREET

JOHN GREENLEAF WHITTIER

THOMAS BUCHANAN READ

EMILY DICKINSON

1830–1886

1

I taste a liquor never brewed —
From Tankards scooped in Pearl —
Not all the Vats upon the Rhine
Yield such an alcohol!

Inebriate of Air — am I —
And Debauchee of Dew —
Reeling — through endless summer days—
From inns of Molten Blue —

When "Landlords" turn the drunken Bee
Out of the Foxglove's door —
When Butterflies — renounce their "drams"—
I shall but drink the more!

Till Seraphs swing their snowy Hats —
And Saints — to windows run —
To see the little Tippler
Leaning against the — Sun —

2

Wild Nights — Wild Nights!
Were I with thee
Wild Nights should be
Our luxury!

Futile — the Winds —
To a Heart in port —
Done with the Compass —
Done with the Chart!

Rowing in Eden —
Ah, the Sea!
Might I but moor — Tonight —
In Thee!

3

"Hope" is the thing with feathers —
That perches in the soul —
And sings the tune without the words —
And never stops — at all —

And sweetest — in the Gale — is heard —
And sore must be the storm —
That could abash the little Bird
That kept so many warm —

I've heard it in the chillest land —
And on the strangest Sea —
Yet, never, in Extremity,
It asked a crumb — of Me.

4

I felt a Funeral, in my Brain,
And Mourners to and fro
Kept treading — treading — till it seemed
That Sense was breaking through —

And when they all were seated,
A Service, like a Drum —
Kept beating — beating — till I thought
My Mind was going numb —

And then I heard them lift a Box
And creak across my Soul
With those same Boots of Lead, again,
Then Space — began to toll,

As all the Heavens were a Bell,
And Being, but an Ear,

And I, and Silence, some strange Race
Wrecked, solitary, here —

And then a Plank in Reason, broke,
And I dropped down, and down —
And hit a World, at every plunge,
And Finished knowing — then —

5

I'm Nobody! Who are you?
Are you — Nobody — too?
Then there's a pair of us!
Don't tell! they'd advertise — you know.

How dreary — to be — Somebody!
How public — like a Frog —
To tell one's name — the livelong June —
To an admiring Bog!

6

The Soul selects her own Society —
Then — shuts the Door —
To her divine Majority —
Present no more —

Unmoved — she notes the Chariots —
pausing —
At her low Gate —
Unmoved — an Emperor be kneeling
Upon her Mat —

I've known her — from an ample nation —
Choose One —
Then — close the Valves of her attention —
Like Stone —

7

A Bird came down the Walk —
He did not know I saw —
He bit an Angleworm in halves
And ate the fellow, raw,

And then he drank a Dew
From a convenient Grass —
And then hopped sidewise to the Wall
To let a Beetle pass —

He glanced with rapid eyes
That hurried all around —
They looked like frightened Beads,
I thought —
He stirred his Velvet Head

Like one in danger, Cautious,
I offered him a Crumb
And he unrolled his feathers
And rowed him softer home —

Than Oars divide the Ocean,
Too silver for a seam —
Or Butterflies, off Banks of Noon
Leap, plashless as they swim.

8

I measure every Grief I meet
With narrow, probing, Eyes —
I wonder if It weighs like Mine —
Or has an Easier size.

I wonder if They bore it long —
Or did it just begin —
I could not tell the Date of Mine —
It feels so old a pain —

I wonder if it hurts to live —
And if They have to try —
And whether — could They choose
between —
It would not be — to die —

I note that Some — gone patient long —
At length, renew their smile —
An imitation of a Light
That has so little Oil —

I wonder if when Years have piled —
Some Thousands — on the Harm —
That hurt them early — such a lapse
Could give them any Balm —

Or would they go on aching still
Through Centuries of Nerve —
Enlightened to a larger Pain —
In Contrast with the Love —

The Grieved — are many — I am told —
There is the various Cause —
Death — is but one — and comes but once—
And only nails the eyes —

There's Grief of Want — and Grief of Cold—
A sort they call "Despair" —
There's Banishment from native Eyes —
In sight of Native Air —

And though I may not guess the kind —
Correctly — yet to me
A piercing Comfort it affords
In passing Calvary —

To note the fashions — of the Cross —
And how they're mostly worn —
Still fascinated to presume
That Some — are like My Own —

9

Because I could not stop for Death —
He kindly stopped for me —
The Carriage held but just Ourselves —
And Immortality.

We slowly drove — He knew no haste,
And I had put away
My labor and my leisure too,
For His Civility —

We passed the School, where Children strove
At recess — in the ring —
We passed the Fields of Gazing Grain —
We passed the Setting Sun —

Or rather — He passed Us —
The Dews drew quivering and chill —
For only Gossamer, my Gown —
My Tippet — only Tulle —

We paused before a House that seemed
A Swelling of the Ground —
The Roof was scarcely visible —
The Cornice — in the Ground —

Since then — 'tis centuries — and yet
Feels shorter than the Day
I first surmised the Horses' Heads
Were toward Eternity —

10

That I did always love
I bring thee Proof
That till I loved
I never lived — Enough —

That I shall love alway —
I argue thee
That love is life —
And life hath Immortality —

This—dost thou doubt—Sweet—
Then have I
Nothing to show
But Calvary —

WALT WHITMAN

1819–1892

11

O CAPTAIN! MY CAPTAIN!

O Captain! my Captain! our fearful trip is done,

The ship has weather'd every rack, the prize we
sought is won,[1]

The port is near, the bells I hear, the people all
exulting,

While follow eyes the steady keel, the vessel
grim and daring;

But O heart! heart! heart!

O the bleeding drops of red,[2]

Where on the deck my Captain lies,

Fallen cold and dead.

O Captain! my Captain! rise up and hear the bells;

---

1 The prize won might be a reference to the abolishment of
slavery. Lincoln had passed the Emancipation Proclamation
in 1863. The slaveholders in the southern states were
unhappy, people in the northern states were skeptical, and
the slaves were jubilant.

2 The poem is about Abraham Lincoln's death. Two years
before this poem was published, John Wilkes, a Confederate
sympathizer, assassinated Lincoln, shooting him in the head.

Rise up—for you the flag is flung—for you the
bugle trills,
For you bouquets and ribbon'd wreaths—for you
the shores a-crowding,
For you they call, the swaying mass, their eager
faces turning;
Here Captain! dear father!
This arm beneath your head!
It is some dream that on the deck,
You've fallen cold and dead.

My Captain does not answer, his lips are pale
and still,
My father does not feel my arm, he has no pulse
nor will,
The ship is anchor'd safe and sound, its voyage
closed and done,
From fearful trip the victor ship comes in with
object won;
Exult O shores, and ring O bells!
But I with mournful tread,
Walk the deck my Captain lies,
Fallen cold and dead.

12

A GLIMPSE

A glimpse through an interstice caught,
Of a crowd of workmen and drivers in a
bar-room around the stove late of a winter
night, and I unremark'd seated in a corner,
Of a youth who loves me and whom I love,
silently approaching and seating himself
near, that he may hold me by the hand,
A long while amid the noises of coming and
going, of drinking and oath and smutty jest,
There we two, content, happy in being together,
speaking little, perhaps not a word.

13

TO A STRANGER

Passing stranger! you do not know how longingly I
look upon you,
You must be he I was seeking, or she I was
seeking, (it comes to me, as of a dream,)
I have somewhere surely lived a life of joy with you,
All is recall'd as we flit by each other, fluid,
affectionate, chaste, matured,
You grew up with me, were a boy with me, or a girl
with me,
I ate with you, and slept with you—your body has
become not yours only, nor left my body mine only,
You give me the pleasure of your eyes, face, flesh,
as we pass—you take of my beard, breast, hands,
in return,
I am not to speak to you—I am to think of you when
I sit alone, or wake at night alone,
I am to wait—I do not doubt I am to meet you again,
I am to see to it that I do not lose you.

14

I SING THE BODY ELECTRIC

1

I sing the body electric,
The armies of those I love engirth me and I engirth
them,
They will not let me off till I go with them, respond
to them,
And discorrupt them, and charge them full with the
charge of the soul.
Was it doubted that those who corrupt their own
bodies conceal themselves?
And if those who defile the living are as bad as they
who defile the dead?
And if the body does not do fully as much as the soul?
And if the body were not the soul, what is the soul?

2

The love of the body of man or woman balks
account, the body itself balks account,

That of the male is perfect, and that of the female is perfect.

The expression of the face balks account,

But the expression of a well-made man appears not only in his face,

It is in his limbs and joints also, it is curiously in the joints of his hips and wrists,

It is in his walk, the carriage of his neck, the flex of his waist and knees, dress does not hide him,

The strong sweet quality he has strikes through the cotton and broadcloth,

To see him pass conveys as much as the best poem, perhaps more,

You linger to see his back, and the back of his neck and shoulder-side.

The sprawl and fulness of babes, the bosoms and heads of women, the folds of their dress, their style as we pass in the street, the contour of their shape downwards,

The swimmer naked in the swimming-bath, seen as he swims throughthe transparent green-shine, or lies with his face up and rolls silently to and from the heave of the water,

The bending forward and backward of rowers in row-boats, the horse-man in his saddle,

Girls, mothers, house-keepers, in all their performances,
The group of laborers seated at noon-time with their open dinner-kettles, and their wives waiting,
The female soothing a child, the farmer's daughter in the garden or cow-yard,
The young fellow hosing corn, the sleigh-driver driving his six horses through the crowd,
The wrestle of wrestlers, two apprentice-boys, quite grown, lusty, good-natured, native-born, out on the vacant lot at sundown after work,
The coats and caps thrown down, the embrace of love and resistance,
The upper-hold and under-hold, the hair rumpled over and blinding the eyes;
The march of firemen in their own costumes, the play of masculine muscle through clean-setting trowsers and waist-straps,
The slow return from the fire, the pause when the bell strikes suddenly again, and the listening on the alert,
The natural, perfect, varied attitudes, the bent head, the curv'd neck and the counting;
Such-like I love—I loosen myself, pass freely, am at the mother's breast with the little child,
Swim with the swimmers, wrestle with wrestlers, march in line with the firemen, and pause, listen, count.

I knew a man, a common farmer, the father of
five sons,
And in them the fathers of sons, and in them the
fathers of sons.
This man was a wonderful vigor, calmness, beauty
of person,
The shape of his head, the pale yellow and white of
his hair and beard, the immeasurable meaning of his
black eyes, the richness and breadth of his manners,
These I used to go and visit him to see, he was
wise also,
He was six feet tall, he was over eighty years old, his sons
were massive, clean, bearded, tan-faced, handsome,
They and his daughters loved him, all who saw him
loved him,
They did not love him by allowance, they loved him
with personal love,
He drank water only, the blood show'd like scarlet
through the clear-brown skin of his face,
He was a frequent gunner and fisher, he sail'd his boat
himself, he had a fine one presented to him by a ship-
joiner, he had fowling-pieces presented to him by
men that loved him,
When he went with his five sons and many grand-sons

to hunt or fish, you would pick him out as the most beautiful and vigorous of the gang,

You would wish long and long to be with him, you would wish to sit by him in the boat that you and he might touch each other.

4

I have perceiv'd that to be with those I like is enough,
To stop in company with the rest at evening is enough,
To be surrounded by beautiful, curious, breathing, laughing flesh is enough,
To pass among them or touch any one, or rest my arm ever so lightly round his or her neck for a moment, what is this then?
I do not ask any more delight, I swim in it as in a sea.
There is something in staying close to men and women and looking on them, and in the contact and odor of them, that pleases the soul well,
All things please the soul, but these please the soul well.

5

This is the female form,
A divine nimbus exhales from it from head to foot,
It attracts with fierce undeniable attraction,
I am drawn by its breath as if I were no more than a helpless vapor, all falls aside but myself and it,

Books, art, religion, time, the visible and solid earth, and what was expected of heaven or fear'd of hell, are now consumed,

Mad filaments, ungovernable shoots play out of it, the response likewise ungovernable,

Hair, bosom, hips, bend of legs, negligent falling hands all diffused, mine too diffused,

Ebb stung by the flow and flow stung by the ebb, love-flesh swelling and deliciously aching,

Limitless limpid jets of love hot and enormous, quivering jelly of love, white-blow and delirious nice,

Bridegroom night of love working surely and softly into the prostrate dawn,

Undulating into the willing and yielding day,

Lost in the cleave of the clasping and sweet-flesh'd day.

This the nucleus—after the child is born of woman, man is born of woman,

This the bath of birth, this the merge of small and large, and the outlet again.

Be not ashamed women, your privilege encloses the rest, and is the exit of the rest,

You are the gates of the body, and you are the gates of the soul.

The female contains all qualities and tempers them,

She is in her place and moves with perfect balance,

She is all things duly veil'd, she is both passive and active,
She is to conceive daughters as well as sons, and sons
as well as daughters.
As I see my soul reflected in Nature,
As I see through a mist, One with inexpressible
completeness, sanity, beauty,
See the bent head and arms folded over the breast, the
Female I see.

6

The male is not less the soul nor more, he too is in his
place,
He too is all qualities, he is action and power,
The flush of the known universe is in him,
Scorn becomes him well, and appetite and defiance
become him well,
The wildest largest passions, bliss that is utmost, sorrow
that is utmost become him well, pride is for him,
The full-spread pride of man is calming and excellent
to the soul,
Knowledge becomes him, he likes it always, he brings
every thing to the test of himself,
Whatever the survey, whatever the sea and the sail he
strikes soundings at last only here,
(Where else does he strike soundings except here?)

The man's body is sacred and the woman's body
is sacred,
No matter who it is, it is sacred—is it the meanest
one in the laborers' gang?
Is it one of the dull-faced immigrants just landed
on the wharf?
Each belongs here or anywhere just as much as
the well-off, just as much as you,
Each has his or her place in the procession.
(All is a procession,
The universe is a procession with measured
and perfect motion.)
Do you know so much yourself that you call
the meanest ignorant?
Do you suppose you have a right to a good sight,
and he or she has no right to a sight?
Do you think matter has cohered together from
its diffuse float, and the soil is on the surface, and
water runs and vegetation sprouts,
For you only, and not for him and her?

7

A man's body at auction,
(For before the war I often go to the slave-mart
and watch the sale,)

I help the auctioneer, the sloven does not half know his business.

Gentlemen look on this wonder,

Whatever the bids of the bidders they cannot be high enough for it,

For it the globe lay preparing quintillions of years without one animal or plant,

For it the revolving cycles truly and steadily roll'd.

In this head the all-baffling brain,

In it and below it the makings of heroes.

Examine these limbs, red, black, or white, they are cunning in tendon and nerve,

They shall be stript that you may see them.

Exquisite senses, life-lit eyes, pluck, volition,

Flakes of breast-muscle, pliant backbone and neck, flesh not flabby, good-sized arms and legs,

And wonders within there yet.

Within there runs blood,

The same old blood! the same red-running blood!

There swells and jets a heart, there all passions, desires, reachings, aspirations,

(Do you think they are not there because they are not express'd in parlors and lecture-rooms?)

This is not only one man, this the father of those who shall be fathers in their turns,

In him the start of populous states and rich republics,
Of him countless immortal lives with countless embodiments and enjoyments.
How do you know who shall come from the offspring of his offspring through the centuries?
(Who might you find you have come from yourself, if you could trace back through the centuries?)

8

A woman's body at auction,
She too is not only herself, she is the teeming mother of mothers,
She is the bearer of them that shall grow and be mates to the mothers.
Have you ever loved the body of a woman?
Have you ever loved the body of a man?
Do you not see that these are exactly the same to all in all nations and times all over the earth?
If anything is sacred the human body is sacred,
And the glory and sweet of a man is the token of manhood untainted,
And in man or woman a clean, strong, firm-fibred body, is more beautiful than the most beautiful face.
Have you seen the fool that corrupted his own live body? or the fool that corrupted her own live body?

For they do not conceal themselves, and cannot conceal themselves.

9

O my body! I dare not desert the likes of you in other men and women, nor the likes of the parts of you,
I believe the likes of you are to stand or fall with the likes of the soul, (and that they are the soul,)
I believe the likes of you shall stand or fall with my poems, and that they are my poems,
Man's, woman's, child, youth's, wife's, husband's, mother's, father's, young man's, young woman's poems,
Head, neck, hair, ears, drop and tympan of the ears,
Eyes, eye-fringes, iris of the eye, eyebrows, and the waking or sleeping of the lids,
Mouth, tongue, lips, teeth, roof of the mouth, jaws, and the jaw-hinges,
Nose, nostrils of the nose, and the partition,
Cheeks, temples, forehead, chin, throat, back of the neck, neck-slue,
Strong shoulders, manly beard, scapula, hind-shoulders, and the ample side-round of the chest,
Upper-arm, armpit, elbow-socket, lower-arm, arm-sinews, arm-bones,

Wrist and wrist-joints, hand, palm, knuckles, thumb, forefinger, finger-joints, finger-nails,
Broad breast-front, curling hair of the breast, breast-bone, breast-side,
Ribs, belly, backbone, joints of the backbone,
Hips, hip-sockets, hip-strength, inward and outward round, man-balls, man-root,
Strong set of thighs, well carrying the trunk above,
Leg-fibres, knee, knee-pan, upper-leg, under-leg,
Ankles, instep, foot-ball, toes, toe-joints, the heel;
All attitudes, all the shapeliness, all the belongings of my or your body or of any one's body, male or female,
The lung-sponges, the stomach-sac, the bowels sweet and clean,
The brain in its folds inside the skull-frame,
Sympathies, heart-valves, palate-valves, sexuality, maternity,
Womanhood, and all that is a woman, and the man that comes from woman,
The womb, the teats, nipples, breast-milk, tears, laughter, weeping, love-looks, love-perturbations and risings,
The voice, articulation, language, whispering, shouting aloud,

Food, drink, pulse, digestion, sweat, sleep, walking, swimming,

Poise on the hips, leaping, reclining, embracing, arm-curving and tightening,

The continual changes of the flex of the mouth, and around the eyes,

The skin, the sunburnt shade, freckles, hair,

The curious sympathy one feels when feeling with the hand the naked meat of the body,

The circling rivers the breath, and breathing it in and out,

The beauty of the waist, and thence of the hips, and thence downward toward the knees,

The thin red jellies within you or within me, the bones and the marrow in the bones,

The exquisite realization of health;

O I say these are not the parts and poems of the body only, but of the soul,

O I say now these are the soul!

15

ONE'S-SELF I SING

One's-self I sing, a simple separate person,
Yet utter the word Democratic, the word
En-Masse.

Of physiology from top to toe I sing,
Not physiognomy alone nor brain alone is
worthy for the Muse,
I say the Form complete is worthier far,
The Female equally with the Male I sing.

Of Life immense in passion, pulse, and
power,
Cheerful, for freest action form'd under
the laws divine,
The Modern Man I sing.

16

I DREAM'D IN A DREAM

I dream'd in a dream I saw a city invincible to
the attacks of the whole of the rest of the earth,
I dream'd that was the new city of Friends,
Nothing was greater there than the quality of
robust love, it led the rest,
It was seen every hour in the actions of the men
of that city,
And in all their looks and words.

17

PIONEERS! O PIONEERS!

Come my tan-faced children,
Follow well in order, get your weapons ready,
Have you your pistols? have you your sharp-edged
axes?
    Pioneers! O pioneers!
For we cannot tarry here,
We must march my darlings, we must bear the
brunt of danger,
We the youthful sinewy races, all the rest on us
depend,
    Pioneers! O pioneers!
O you youths, Western youths,
So impatient, full of action, full of manly pride
and friendship,
Plain I see you Western youths, see you tramping
with the foremost,
    Pioneers! O pioneers!
Have the elder races halted?

Do they droop and end their lesson, wearied over
there beyond the seas?
We take up the task eternal, and the burden and
the lesson,
    Pioneers! O pioneers!
All the past we leave behind,
We debouch upon a newer mightier world,
varied world,
Fresh and strong the world we seize, world of labor
and the march,
    Pioneers! O pioneers!
We detachments steady throwing,
Down the edges, through the passes, up the
mountains steep,
Conquering, holding, daring, venturing as we go
the unknown ways,
    Pioneers! O pioneers!
We primeval forests felling,
We the rivers stemming, vexing we and piercing
deep the mines within,
We the surface broad surveying, we the virgin
soil upheaving,
    Pioneers! O pioneers!
Colorado men are we,
From the peaks gigantic, from the great sierras
and the high plateaus,

From the mine and from the gully, from the hunting
trail we come,
    Pioneers! O pioneers!
From Nebraska, from Arkansas,
Central inland race are we, from Missouri, with the
continental blood intervein'd,
All the hands of comrades clasping, all the Southern,
all the Northern,
    Pioneers! O pioneers!

O resistless restless race!
O beloved race in all! O my breast aches with tender
love for all!
O I mourn and yet exult, I am rapt with love for all,
    Pioneers! O pioneers!

Raise the mighty mother mistress,
Waving high the delicate mistress, over all the starry
mistress, (bend your heads all,)
Raise the fang'd and warlike mistress, stern, impassive,
weapon'd mistress,
    Pioneers! O pioneers!

See my children, resolute children,
By those swarms upon our rear we must never yield
or falter,
Ages back in ghostly millions frowning there behind
us urging,
    Pioneers! O pioneers!

On and on the compact ranks,
With accessions ever waiting, with the places of the
dead quickly fill'd,

Through the battle, through defeat, moving yet and
never stopping,
    Pioneers! O pioneers!
O to die advancing on!
Are there some of us to droop and die? has the
hour come?
Then upon the march we fittest die, soon and sure
the gap is fill'd.
    Pioneers! O pioneers!
All the pulses of the world,
Falling in they beat for us, with the Western
movement beat,
Holding single or together, steady moving to the
front, all for us,
    Pioneers! O pioneers!
Life's involv'd and varied pageants,
All the forms and shows, all the workmen at
their work,
All the seamen and the landsmen, all the masters
with their slaves,
    Pioneers! O pioneers!
All the hapless silent lovers,
All the prisoners in the prisons, all the righteous
and the wicked,
All the joyous, all the sorrowing, all the living, all
the dying,
    Pioneers! O pioneers!
I too with my soul and body,
We, a curious trio, picking, wandering on our way,

Through these shores amid the shadows, with the
apparitions pressing,
    Pioneers! O pioneers!
Lo, the darting bowling orb!
Lo, the brother orbs around, all the clustering suns
and planets,
All the dazzling days, all the mystic nights with dreams,
    Pioneers! O pioneers!
These are of us, they are with us,
All for primal needed work, while the followers
there in embryo wait behind,
We to-day's procession heading, we the route for
travel clearing,
    Pioneers! O pioneers!
O you daughters of the West!
O you young and elder daughters! O you mothers
and you wives!
Never must you be divided, in our ranks you
move united,
    Pioneers! O pioneers!
Minstrels latent on the prairies!
(Shrouded bards of other lands, you may rest, you
have done your work,)
Soon I hear you coming warbling, soon you rise
and tramp amid us,
    Pioneers! O pioneers!
Not for delectations sweet,
Not the cushion and the slipper, not the peaceful
and the studious,

Not the riches safe and palling, not for us the
tame enjoyment,
    Pioneers! O pioneers!
Do the feasters gluttonous feast?
Do the corpulent sleepers sleep? have they lock'd
and bolted doors?
Still be ours the diet hard, and the blanket on
the ground,
    Pioneers! O pioneers!
Has the night descended?
Was the road of late so toilsome? did we stop
discouraged nodding on our way?
Yet a passing hour I yield you in your tracks to
pause oblivious,
    Pioneers! O pioneers!
Till with sound of trumpet,
Far, far off the daybreak call—hark! how loud
and clear I hear it wind,
Swift! to the head of the army!—swift! spring
to your places,
    Pioneers! O pioneers!

18

A NOISELESS
PATIENT SPIDER

A noiseless patient spider,
I mark'd where on a little promontory
it stood isolated,
Mark'd how to explore the vacant vast
surrounding,
It launch'd forth filament, filament,
filament out of itself,
Ever unreeling them, ever tirelessly
speeding them.
And you O my soul where you stand,
Surrounded, detached, in measureless
oceans of space,
Ceaselessly musing, venturing, throwing,
seeking the spheres to connect them,
Till the bridge you will need be form'd,
till the ductile anchor hold,
Till the gossamer thread you fling catch
somewhere, O my soul.

19

O ME! O LIFE!

O me! O life! of the questions of these recurring,
Of the endless trains of the faithless, of cities
fill'd with the foolish,
Of myself forever reproaching myself, (for who
more foolish than I, and who more faithless?)
Of eyes that vainly crave the light, of the objects
mean, of the struggle ever renew'd,
Of the poor results of all, of the plodding and
sordid crowds I see around me,
Of the empty and useless years of the rest, with
the rest me intertwined,
The question, O me! so sad, recurring—What
good amid these, O me, O life?

Answer.
That you are here—that life exists and identity,
That the powerful play goes on, and you may
contribute a verse.

20

THE VOICE OF THE RAIN

And who art thou? said I to the soft-falling
shower,
Which, strange to tell, gave me an answer, as
here translated:
I am the Poem of Earth, said the voice of the rain,
Eternal I rise impalpable out of the land and the
bottomless sea,
Upward to heaven, whence, vaguely form'd,
altogether changed, and yet the same,
I descend to lave the drouths, atomies, dust-
layers of the globe,
And all that in them without me were seeds only,
latent, unborn;
And forever, by day and night, I give back life to
my own origin, and make pure and beautify it;
(For song, issuing from its birth-place, after
fulfilment, wandering,
Reck'd or unreck'd, duly with love returns.)

ROBERT
FROST

1874–1963

21

THE ROAD NOT TAKEN

Two roads diverged in a yellow wood,
And sorry I could not travel both[3]
And be one traveler, long I stood
And looked down one as far as I could
To where it bent in the undergrowth;

Then took the other, as just as fair,
And having perhaps the better claim,
Because it was grassy and wanted wear;
Though as for that the passing there
Had worn them really about the same,

And both that morning equally lay
In leaves no step had trodden black.
Oh, I kept the first for another day!

---

3 While walking with Frost, his friend, Edward Thomas
   would often express regret on not traversing a different
   path. This everyday act was then transformed into a poem.

Yet knowing how way leads on to way,
I doubted if I should ever come back.

I shall be telling this with a sigh
Somewhere ages and ages hence:

Two roads diverged in a wood, and I—
I took the one less travelled by,[4]
And that has made all the difference.

---

4 Though it is not exactly clear what Frost meant by this, the
common interpretation has come out to be that Frost is
talking about his career choice here. He decided to be a
poet, a profession not opted for by many. But in choosing
to be a poet, he has earned himself a name.

22

STOPPING BY WOODS
ON A SNOWY EVENING

Whose woods these are I think I know.
His house is in the village though;
He will not see me stopping here
To watch his woods fill up with snow.

My little horse must think it queer
To stop without a farmhouse near
Between the woods and frozen lake
The darkest evening of the year.

He gives his harness bells a shake
To ask if there is some mistake.
The only other sound's the sweep
Of easy wind and downy flake.

The woods are lovely, dark and deep,
But I have promises to keep,
And miles to go before I sleep,
And miles to go before I sleep.

23

BIRCHES

When I see birches bend to left and right
Across the lines of straighter darker trees,
I like to think some boy's been swinging them.
But swinging doesn't bend them down to stay.
Ice-storms do that. Often you must have seen them
Loaded with ice a sunny winter morning
After a rain. They click upon themselves
As the breeze rises, and turn many-coloured
As the stir cracks and crazes their enamel.
Soon the sun's warmth makes them shed crystal shells
Shattering and avalanching on the snow-crust—
Such heaps of broken glass to sweep away You'd
think the inner dome of heaven had fallen.
They are dragged to the withered bracken by the load,
And they seem not to break; though once they are bowed
So low for long, they never right themselves:
You may see their trunks arching in the woods

Years afterwards, trailing their leaves on the ground,
Like girls on hands and knees that throw their hair
Before them over their heads to dry in the sun.
But I was going to say when Truth broke in
With all her matter-of-fact about the ice-storm,
I should prefer to have some boy bend them
As he went out and in to fetch the cows—
Some boy too far from town to learn baseball,
Whose only play was what he found himself,
Summer or winter, and could play alone.
One by one he subdued his father's trees
By riding them down over and over again
Until he took the stiffness out of them,
And not one but hung limp, not one was left
For him to conquer. He learned all there was
To learn about not launching out too soon
And so not carrying the tree away
Clear to the ground. He always kept his poise
To the top branches, climbing carefully
With the same pains you use to fill a cup
Up to the brim, and even above the brim.
Then he flung outward, feet first, with a swish,
Kicking his way down through the air to the ground.
So was I once myself a swinger of birches.
And so I dream of going back to be.

It's when I'm weary of considerations,
And life is too much like a pathless wood
Where your face burns and tickles with the cobwebs
Broken across it, and one eye is weeping
From a twig's having lashed across it open.
I'd like to get away from earth awhile
And then come back to it and begin over.
May no fate wilfully misunderstand me
And half grant what I wish and snatch me away
Not to return. Earth's the right place for love:
I don't know where it's likely to go better.
I'd like to go by climbing a birch tree,
And climb black branches up a snow-white trunk
Toward heaven, till the tree could bear no more,
But dipped its top and set me down again.
That would be good both going and coming back.
One could do worse than be a swinger of birches.

24

AFTER APPLE PICKING

My long two-pointed ladder's sticking
through a tree
Toward heaven still,
And there's a barrel that I didn't fill
Beside it, and there may be two or three
Apples I didn't pick upon some bough.
But I am done with apple-picking now.
Essence of winter sleep is on the night,
The scent of apples: I am drowsing off.
I cannot rub the strangeness from my sight
I got from looking through a pane of glass
I skimmed this morning from the
drinking trough
And held against the world of hoary grass.
It melted, and I let it fall and break.
But I was well
Upon my way to sleep before it fell,
And I could tell

What form my dreaming was about to take.
Magnified apples appear and disappear,
Stem end and blossom end,
And every fleck of russet showing clear.
My instep arch not only keeps the ache,
It keeps the pressure of a ladder-round.
I feel the ladder sway as the boughs bend.
And I keep hearing from the cellar bin
The rumbling sound
Of load on load of apples coming in.
For I have had too much
Of apple-picking: I am overtired
Of the great harvest I myself desired.
There were ten thousand thousand fruit to touch,
Cherish in hand, lift down, and not let fall.
For all
That struck the earth,
No matter if not bruised or spiked with stubble,
Went surely to the cider-apple heap
As of no worth.
One can see what will trouble
This sleep of mine, whatever sleep it is.
Were he not gone,
The woodchuck could say whether it's like his
Long sleep, as I describe its coming on,
Or just some human sleep.

25

INTO MY OWN

One of my wishes is that those dark trees,
So old and firm they scarcely show the breeze,
Were not, as 'twere, the merest mask of gloom,
But stretched away unto the edge of doom.

I should not be withheld but that some day
Into their vastness I should steal away,
Fearless of ever finding open land,
Or highway where the slow wheel pours
the sand.

I do not see why I should e'er turn back,
Or those should not set forth upon my track
To overtake me, who should miss me here
And long to know if still I held them dear.

They would not find me changed from him
they knew—
Only more sure of all I thought was true.

26

HOME BURIAL

He saw her from the bottom of the stairs
Before she saw him. She was starting down,
Looking back over her shoulder at some fear.
She took a doubtful step and then undid it
To raise herself and look again. He spoke
Advancing toward her: "What is it you see
From up there always—for I want to know."
She turned and sank upon her skirts at that,
And her face changed from terrified to dull.
He said to gain time: "What is it you see?"
Mounting until she cowered under him.
"I will find out now—you must tell me, dear."
She, in her place, refused him any help
With the least stiffening of her neck and silence.
She let him look, sure that he wouldn't see,
Blind creature; and a while he didn't see.
But at last he murmured, "Oh," and again, "Oh."

"What is it—what?" she said.
"Just that I see."

"You don't," she challenged. "Tell me what it is."

"The wonder is I didn't see at once.
I never noticed it from here before.
I must be wonted to it—that's the reason.
The little graveyard where my people are!
So small the window frames the whole of it.
Not so much larger than a bedroom, is it?
There are three stones of slate and one of marble,
Broad-shouldered little slabs there in the sunlight
On the sidehill. We haven't to mind those.
But I understand: it is not the stones,
But the child's mound—"

"Don't, don't, don't, don't," she cried.

She withdrew shrinking from beneath his arm
That rested on the banister, and slid downstairs;
And turned on him with such a daunting look,
He said twice over before he knew himself:
"Can't a man speak of his own child he's lost?"

"Not you! Oh, where's my hat? Oh, I don't need it!
I must get out of here. I must get air.
I don't know rightly whether any man can."

"Amy! Don't go to someone else this time.
Listen to me. I won't come down the stairs."
He sat and fixed his chin between his fists.
"There's something I should like to ask you, dear."

"You don't know how to ask it."

"Help me, then."

Her fingers moved the latch for all reply.

"My words are nearly always an offence.
I don't know how to speak of anything
So as to please you. But I might be taught
I should suppose. I can't say I see how.
A man must partly give up being a man
With women-folk. We could have some arrangement
By which I'd bind myself to keep hands off
Anything special you're a-mind to name.
Though I don't like such things 'twixt those that love.
Two that don't love can't live together without them.

But two that do can't live together with them."
She moved the latch a little. "Don't—don't go.
Don't carry it to someone else this time.
Tell me about it if it's something human.
Let me into your grief. I'm not so much
Unlike other folks as your standing there
Apart would make me out. Give me my chance.
I do think, though, you overdo it a little.
What was it brought you up to think it the thing
To take your mother-loss of a first child
So inconsolably—in the face of love.
You'd think his memory might be satisfied—"

"There you go sneering now!"

"I'm not, I'm not!
You make me angry. I'll come down to you.
God, what a woman! And it's come to this,
A man can't speak of his own child that's dead."
"You can't because you don't know how.
If you had any feelings, you that dug
With your own hand—how could you?—his little
grave;
I saw you from that very window there,
Making the gravel leap and leap in air,

Leap up, like that, like that, and land so lightly
And roll back down the mound beside the hole.
I thought, Who is that man? I didn't know you.
And I crept down the stairs and up the stairs
To look again, and still your spade kept lifting.
Then you came in. I heard your rumbling voice
Out in the kitchen, and I don't know why,
But I went near to see with my own eyes.
You could sit there with the stains on your shoes
Of the fresh earth from your own baby's grave
And talk about your everyday concerns.
You had stood the spade up against the wall
Outside there in the entry, for I saw it."

"I shall laugh the worst laugh I ever laughed.
I'm cursed. God, if I don't believe I'm cursed."
"I can repeat the very words you were saying.

'Three foggy mornings and one rainy day
Will rot the best birch fence a man can build.'
Think of it, talk like that at such a time!
What had how long it takes a birch to rot
To do with what was in the darkened parlour?
You couldn't care! The nearest friends can go
With anyone to death, comes so far short

They might as well not try to go at all.
No, from the time when one is sick to death,
One is alone, and he dies more alone.
Friends make pretence of following to the grave,
But before one is in it, their minds are turned
And making the best of their way back to life
And living people, and things they understand.
But the world's evil. I won't have grief so
If I can change it. Oh, I won't, I won't!"

"There, you have said it all and you feel better.
You won't go now. You're crying. Close the door.
The heart's gone out of it: why keep it up?
Amy! There's someone coming down the road!"

"You—oh, you think the talk is all. I must go—
Somewhere out of this house. How can I make
you—"

"If—you—do!" She was opening the door wider.
"Where do you mean to go? First tell me that.
I'll follow and bring you back by force. I will!—"

27

OUT, OUT . . .

The buzz-saw snarled and rattled in the yard
And made dust and dropped stove-length sticks
of wood,
Sweet-scented stuff when the breeze drew across it.
And from there those that lifted eyes could count
Five mountain ranges one behind the other
Under the sunset far into Vermont.
And the saw snarled and rattled, snarled and rattled,
As it ran light, or had to bear a load.
And nothing happened: day was all but done.
Call it a day, I wish they might have said
To please the boy by giving him the half hour
That a boy counts so much when saved from work.
His sister stood beside them in her apron
To tell them "Supper." At the word, the saw,
As if to prove saws knew what supper meant,
Leaped out at the boy's hand, or seemed to leap—
He must have given the hand. However it was,

Neither refused the meeting. But the hand!
The boy's first outcry was a rueful laugh.
As he swung toward them holding up the hand
Half in appeal, but half as if to keep
The life from spilling. Then the boy saw all—
Since he was old enough to know, big boy
Doing a man's work, though a child at heart—
He saw all spoiled. "Don't let him cut my hand off—
The doctor, when he comes. Don't let him, sister!"
So. But the hand was gone already.
The doctor put him in the dark of ether.
He lay and puffed his lips out with his breath.
And then—the watcher at his pulse took fright.
No one believed. They listened at his heart.
Little—less—nothing!—and that ended it.
No more to build on there. And they, since they
Were not the one dead, turned to their affairs.

28

MENDING WALL

Something there is that doesn't love a wall,
That sends the frozen-ground-swell under it,
And spills the upper boulders in the sun;
And makes gaps even two can pass abreast.
The work of hunters is another thing:
I have come after them and made repair
Where they have left not one stone on a stone,
But they would have the rabbit out of hiding,
To please the yelping dogs. The gaps I mean,
No one has seen them made or heard them made,
But at spring mending-time we find them there.
I let my neighbour know beyond the hill;
And on a day we meet to walk the line
And set the wall between us once again.
We keep the wall between us as we go.
To each the boulders that have fallen to each.
And some are loaves and some so nearly balls

We have to use a spell to make them balance:
"Stay where you are until our backs are turned!"
We wear our fingers rough with handling them.
Oh, just another kind of out-door game,
One on a side. It comes to little more:
There where it is we do not need the wall:
He is all pine and I am apple orchard.
My apple trees will never get across
And eat the cones under his pines, I tell him.
He only says, "Good fences make good
neighbours."
Spring is the mischief in me, and I wonder
If I could put a notion in his head:
"*Why* do they make good neighbours? Isn't it
Where there are cows? But here there are no
cows.
Before I built a wall I'd ask to know
What I was walling in or walling out,
And to whom I was like to give offence.
Something there is that doesn't love a wall,
That wants it down." I could say "Elves" to him,
But it's not elves exactly, and I'd rather
He said it for himself. I see him there
Bringing a stone grasped firmly by the top

In each hand, like an old-stone savage armed.
He moves in darkness as it seems to me,
Not of woods only and the shade of trees.
He will not go behind his father's saying,
And he likes having thought of it so well
He says again, "Good fences make good neighbours."

29

HYLA BROOK

By June our brook's run out of song and speed.
Sought for much after that, it will be found
Either to have gone groping underground
(And taken with it all the Hyla breed
That shouted in the mist a month ago,
Like ghost of sleigh-bells in a ghost of snow)—
Or flourished and come up in jewel-weed,
Weak foliage that is blown upon and bent
Even against the way its waters went.
Its bed is left a faded paper sheet
Of dead leaves stuck together by the heat—
A brook to none but who remember long.
This as it will be seen is other far
Than with brooks taken otherwhere in song.
We love the things we love for what they are.

30

TO THE THAWING WIND

Come with rain, O loud Southwester!
Bring the singer, bring the nester;
Give the buried flower a dream;
Make the settled snow-bank steam;
Find the brown beneath the white;
But whate'er you do to-night,
Bathe my window, make it flow,
Melt it as the ice will go;
Melt the glass and leave the sticks
Like a hermit's crucifix;
Burst into my narrow stall;
Swing the picture on the wall;
Run the rattling pages o'er;
Scatter poems on the floor;
Turn the poet out of door.

EDGAR
ALLAN POE

1809–1849

31

ANNABEL LEE

It was many and many a year ago,
In a kingdom by the sea,
That a maiden there lived whom you may know
By the name of Annabel Lee;
And this maiden she lived with no other thought
Than to love and be loved by me.

I was a child and *she* was a child,
In this kingdom by the sea,
But we loved with a love that was more than love—
I and my Annabel Lee;
With a love that the wingèd seraphs of heaven
Coveted her and me.

And this was the reason that, long ago,
In this kingdom by the sea,
A wind blew out of a cloud, chilling
My beautiful Annabel Lee;
So that her highborn kinsman came

And bore her away from me,
To shut her up in a sepulchre
In this kingdom by the sea.

The angels, not half so happy in heaven,
Went envying her and me—
Yes!—that was the reason (as all men know,
In this kingdom by the sea)
That the wind came out of the cloud by night,
Chilling and killing my Annabel Lee.

But our love it was stronger by far than the love
Of those who were older than we—
Of many far wiser than we—
And neither the angels in heaven above
Nor the demons down under the sea
Can ever dissever my soul from the soul
Of the beautiful Annabel Lee.

For the moon never beams, without bringing
me dreams
Of the beautiful Annabel Lee;
And the stars never rise, but I feel the bright eyes
Of the beautiful Annabel Lee;
And so, all the night-tide, I lie down by the side
Of my darling—my darling—my life and my bride,
In her sepulchre there by the sea,
In her tomb by the sounding sea.

32

TO HELEN

Helen, thy beauty is to me
Like those Nicéan barks of yore,
That gently, o'er a perfumed sea,
The weary, way-worn wanderer bore
To his own native shore.

On desperate seas long wont to roam,
Thy hyacinth hair, thy classic face,
Thy Naiad airs have brought me home
To the glory that was Greece,
And the grandeur that was Rome.

Lo! in yon brilliant window-niche
How statue-like I see thee stand,
The agate lamp within thy hand!
A Psyche from the regions which
Are Holy-Land!

33

THE RAVEN

Once upon a midnight dreary, while I pondered, weak and weary,
Over many a quaint and curious volume of forgotten lore—
While I nodded, nearly napping, suddenly there came a tapping,
As of some one gently rapping, rapping at my chamber door.
"'Tis some visitor," I muttered, "tapping at my chamber door—
Only this and nothing more."

Ah, distinctly I remember it was in the bleak December;
And each separate dying ember wrought its ghost upon the floor.
Eagerly I wished the morrow;—vainly I had sought to borrow

From my books surcease of sorrow—sorrow for
the lost Lenore—
For the rare and radiant maiden whom the angels
name Lenore—
Nameless *here* for evermore.

And the silken, sad, uncertain rustling of each
purple curtain
Thrilled me—filled me with fantastic terrors
never felt before;
So that now, to still the beating of my heart, I
stood repeating
"'Tis some visitor entreating entrance at my
chamber door—
Some late visitor entreating entrance at my
chamber door;—
This it is and nothing more."

Presently my soul grew stronger; hesitating
then no longer,
"Sir," said I, "or Madam, truly your forgiveness
I implore;
But the fact is I was napping, and so gently you
came rapping,
And so faintly you came tapping, tapping at my
chamber door,
That I scarce was sure I heard you"—here I
opened wide the door;—
Darkness there and nothing more.

Deep into that darkness peering, long I stood there wondering, fearing,

Doubting, dreaming dreams no mortal ever dared to dream before;

But the silence was unbroken, and the stillness gave no token,

And the only word there spoken was the whispered word, "Lenore?"

This I whispered, and an echo murmured back the word, "Lenore!"—

Merely this and nothing more.

Back into the chamber turning, all my soul within me burning,

Soon again I heard a tapping somewhat louder than before.

"Surely," said I, "surely that is something at my window lattice;

Let me see, then, what thereat is, and this mystery explore—

Let my heart be still a moment and this mystery explore;—

'Tis the wind and nothing more!"

Open here I flung the shutter, when, with many a flirt and flutter,

In there stepped a stately Raven of the saintly days of yore;

Not the least obeisance made he; not a minute
stopped or stayed he;
But, with mien of lord or lady, perched above my
chamber door—
Perched upon a bust of Pallas[5] just above my
chamber door—
Perched, and sat, and nothing more.

Then this ebony bird beguiling my sad fancy
into smiling,
By the grave and stern decorum of the
countenance it wore,
"Though thy crest be shorn and shaven, thou,"
I said,
"art sure no craven,
Ghastly grim and ancient Raven wandering
from the Nightly shore—
Tell me what thy lordly name is on the Night's
Plutonian shore!"
Quoth the Raven "Nevermore."

Much I marvelled this ungainly fowl to hear
discourse so plainly,

---

5   Pallas was an epithet given to Athena, the goddess
    of wisdom. That the raven perches on the bust of
    Pallas may serve as an indication to the readers than
    the bird is extraordinary. Though all it is able to say
    is 'Nevermore', it does come at a time when the man
    was expecting to see his dead beloved's ghost.

Though its answer little meaning—little
relevancy bore;
For we cannot help agreeing that no living
human being
Ever yet was blessed with seeing bird above his
chamber door—
Bird or beast upon the sculptured bust above his
chamber door,
With such name as "Nevermore."

But the Raven, sitting lonely on the placid
bust, spoke only
That one word, as if his soul in that one word he
did outpour.
Nothing farther then he uttered—not a feather
then he fluttered—
Till I scarcely more than muttered "Other
friends have flown before—
On the morrow *he* will leave me, as my Hopes
have
flown before."
Then the bird said "Nevermore."

Startled at the stillness broken by reply so aptly
spoken,
"Doubtless," said I, "what it utters is its only
stock and store
Caught from some unhappy master whom
unmerciful Disaster

Followed fast and followed faster till his songs
one burden bore—
Till the dirges of his Hope that melancholy
burden bore
Of 'Never—nevermore.'"

But the Raven still beguiling all my fancy[6] into
smiling,
Straight I wheeled a cushioned seat in front of
bird, and bust and door;
Then, upon the velvet sinking, I betook myself
to linking
Fancy unto fancy, thinking what this ominous
bird of yore—
What this grim, ungainly, ghastly, gaunt, and
ominous bird of yore
Meant in croaking "Nevermore."

This I sat engaged in guessing, but no syllable
expressing
To the fowl whose fiery eyes now burned into my
bosom's core;
This and more I sat divining, with my head at
ease reclining

---

6   An interpretation of the talking bird's existence is that it
    is only in the mind of the man, and is, therefore, not real.
    The grief of Lenore's death is eating away at the man to the
    point of hallucinations. But the fantastical elements are a
    part and parcel of Gothicism, so a talking bird appearing at
    the dead of the night might not be a mere illusion.

On the cushion's velvet lining that the lamp-light gloated o'er,
But whose velvet-violet lining with the lamp-light gloating o'er,
She shall press, ah, nevermore!

Then, methought, the air grew denser, perfumed from an unseen censer
Swung by Seraphim whose foot-falls tinkled on the tufted floor.
"Wretch," I cried, "thy God hath lent thee—by these angels he hath sent thee
Respite—respite and nepenthe from thy memories of Lenore;
Quaff, oh quaff this kind nepenthe and forget this lost Lenore!"
Quoth the Raven "Nevermore."

"Prophet!" said I, "thing of evil!—prophet still, if bird or devil!—
Whether Tempter sent, or whether tempest tossed thee here ashore,
Desolate yet all undaunted, on this desert land enchanted—
On this home by Horror haunted—tell me truly, I implore—
Is there—*is* there balm in Gilead?—tell me—tell me,

I implore!"
Quoth the Raven "Nevermore."

"Prophet!" said I, "thing of evil!—prophet still,
if bird or devil!
By that Heaven that bends above us—by that
God we both adore—
Tell this soul with sorrow laden if, within the
distant Aidenn,
It shall clasp a sainted maiden whom the angels
name Lenore—
Clasp a rare and radiant maiden whom the angels
name Lenore."
Quoth the Raven "Nevermore."

"Be that word our sign of parting, bird or fiend!"
I shrieked, upstarting—
"Get thee back into the tempest and the Night's
Plutonian shore!
Leave no black plume as a token of that lie thy
soul hath spoken!
Leave my loneliness unbroken!—quit the bust
above my door!
Take thy beak from out my heart, and take thy
form from off my door!"
Quoth the Raven "Nevermore."

And the Raven, never flitting, still is
sitting, *still* is sitting

On the pallid bust of Pallas just above my chamber door;

And his eyes have all the seeming of a demon's that is dreaming,

And the lamp-light o'er him streaming throws his shadow on the floor;

And my soul from out that shadow that lies floating on the floor

Shall be lifted—nevermore!

34

THE CITY IN THE SEA

Lo! Death has reared himself a throne
In a strange city lying alone
Far down within the dim West,
Where the good and the bad and the worst
and the best
Have gone to their eternal rest.
There shrines and palaces and towers
(Time-eaten towers that tremble not!)
Resemble nothing that is ours.
Around, by lifting winds forgot,
Resignedly beneath the sky
The melancholy waters lie.

No rays from the holy heaven come down
On the long night-time of that town;
But light from out the lurid sea
Streams up the turrets silently—

Gleams up the pinnacles far and free—
Up domes—up spires—up kingly halls—
Up fanes—up Babylon-like walls—
Up shadowy long-forgotten bowers
Of scultured ivy and stone flowers—
Up many and many a marvelous shrine
Whose wreathed friezes intertwine
The viol, the violet, and the vine.

Resignedly beneath the sky
The melancholy waters lie.
So blend the turrets and shadows there
That all seem pendulous in air,
While from a proud tower in the town
Death looks gigantically down.

There open fanes and gaping graves
Yawn level with the luminous waves;
But not the riches there that lie
In each idol's diamond eye—
Not the gaily-jeweled dead
Tempt the waters from their bed;
For no ripples curl, alas!
Along that wilderness of glass—

No swellings tell that winds may be
Upon some far-off happier sea—
No heavings hint that winds have been
On seas less hideously serene.

But lo, a stir is in the air!
The wave—there is a movement there!
As if the towers had thrown aside,
In slightly sinking, the dull tide—
As if their tops had feebly given
A void within the filmy Heaven.
The waves have now a redder glow—
The hours are breathing faint and low—
And when, amid no earthly moans,
Down, down that town shall settle hence,
Hell, rising from a thousand thrones,
Shall do it reverence.

35

LENORE

Ah, broken is the golden bowl! the spirit
flown forever!
Let the bell toll!—a saintly soul floats on
the Stygian river;
And, Guy De Vere, hast *thou* no tear?—
weep now or never more!
See! on yon drear and rigid bier low lies
thy love, Lenore!
Come! let the burial rite be read—the
funeral song be sung!—
An anthem for the queenliest dead that
ever died so young—
A dirge for her the doubly dead in that
she died so young.

"Wretches! ye loved her for her wealth
and hated her for her pride,
"And when she fell in feeble health, ye
blessed her—that she died!

"How *shall* the ritual, then, be read?—the
requiem how be sung
"By you—by yours, the evil eye,—by yours,
the slanderous tongue
"That did to death the innocent that died,
and died so young?"

Peccavimus; but rave not thus! and let a
Sabbath song
Go up to God so solemnly the dead may
feel so wrong!
The sweet Lenore hath "gone before," with
Hope, that flew beside
Leaving thee wild for the dear child that
should have been thy bride—
For her, the fair and *debonair*, that now so
lowly lies,
The life upon her yellow hair but not within
her eyes—
The life still there, upon her hair—the death
upon her eyes.
"Avaunt! to-night my heart is light. No dirge
will I upraise,
"But waft the angel on her flight with a Paean
of old days!
"Let *no* bell toll!—lest her sweet soul, amid its
hallowed mirth,

"Should catch the note, as it doth float—up
from the damnéd Earth.
"To friends above, from fiends below, the
indignant ghost is riven—
"From Hell unto a high estate far up within
the Heaven—
"From grief and groan, to a golden throne,
beside the King of Heaven."

36

TO ONE IN PARADISE

Thou wast all that to me, love,
For which my soul did pine:
A green isle in the sea, love,
A fountain and a shrine
All wreathed with fairy fruits and
flowers,
And all the flowers were mine.

Ah, dream too bright to last!
Ah, starry Hope, that didst arise
But to be overcast!
A voice from out the Future cries,
"On! on!"—but o'er the Past
(Dim gulf!) my spirit hovering lies
Mute, motionless, aghast.

For, alas! alas! with me
The light of Life is o'er!
No more—no more—no more—

(Such language holds the solemn sea
To the sands upon the shore)
Shall bloom the thunder-blasted tree,
Or the stricken eagle soar.

And all my days are trances,
And all my nightly dreams
Are where thy gray eye glances,
And where thy footstep gleams—
In what ethereal dances,
By what eternal streams.

37

TO MY MOTHER

Because I feel that, in the Heavens above,
The angels, whispering to one another,
Can find among their burning terms of
love—
None so devotional as that of "Mother,"
Therefore by that dear name I long have
called you—
You who are more than mother unto me,
And fill my heart of hearts where Death
installed you
In setting my Virginia's spirit free.
My mother, my own mother, who died early,
Was but the mother of myself; but you
Are mother to the one I loved so dearly,
And thus are dearer than the mother I knew
By that infinity with which my wife
Was dearer to my soul than its soul-life.

38

A DREAM WITHIN A DREAM

Take this kiss upon the brow!
And, in parting from you now,
Thus much let me avow—
You are not wrong, who deem
That my days have been a dream;
Yet if Hope has flown away
In a night, or in a day,
In a vision, or in none,
Is it therefore the less *gone*?
All that we see or seem
Is but a dream within a dream.

I stand amid the roar
Of a surf-tormented shore,
And I hold within my hand
Grains of the golden sand—
How few! yet how they creep

Through my fingers to the deep,
While I weep—while I weep!
O God! can I not grasp
Them with a tighter clasp?
O God! can I not save
One from the pitiless wave?
Is *all* that we see or seem
But a dream within a dream?

39

AL AARAAF

PART I

O! Nothing earthly save the ray
(Thrown back from flowers) of Beauty's eye,
As in those gardens where the day
Springs from the gems of Circassy—
O! nothing earthly save the thrill
Of melody in woodland rill—
Or (music of the passion-hearted)
Joy's voice so peacefully departed
That like the murmur in the shell,
Its echo dwelleth and will dwell—
Oh, nothing of the dross of ours—
Yet all the beauty—all the flowers
That list our Love, and deck our bowers—
Adorn yon world afar, afar—
The wandering star.

'Twas a sweet time for Nesace—for there
Her world lay lolling on the golden air,
Near four bright suns—a temporary rest—
An oasis in desert of the blest.
Away—away—'mid seas of rays that roll
Empyrean splendor o'er th' unchained soul—
The soul that scarce (the billows are so dense)
Can struggle to its destin'd eminence—
To distant spheres, from time to time, she rode,
And late to ours, the favour'd one of God—
But, now, the ruler of an anchor'd realm,
She throws aside the sceptre—leaves the helm,
And, amid incense and high spiritual hymns,
Laves in quadruple light her angel limbs.

Now happiest, loveliest in yon lovely Earth,
Whence sprang the "Idea of Beauty" into birth,
(Falling in wreaths thro' many a startled star,
Like woman's hair 'mid pearls, until, afar,
It lit on hills Achaian, and there dwelt)
She look'd into Infinity—and knelt.
Rich clouds, for canopies, about her curled—
Fit emblems of the model of her world—
Seen but in beauty—not impeding sight

Of other beauty glittering thro' the light—
A wreath that twined each starry form around,
And all the opal'd air in color bound.

All hurriedly she knelt upon a bed
Of flowers: of lilies such as rear'd the head
On the fair Capo Deucato, and sprang
So eagerly around about to hang
Upon the flying footsteps of—deep pride—
Of her who lov'd a mortal—and so died.
The Sephalica, budding with young bees,
Uprear'd its purple stem around her knees:
And gemmy flower, of Trebizond misnam'd—
Inmate of highest stars, where erst it sham'd
All other loveliness: its honied dew
(The fabled nectar that the heathen knew)
Deliriously sweet, was dropp'd from Heaven,
And fell on gardens of the unforgiven
In Trebizond—and on a sunny flower
So like its own above that, to this hour,
It still remaineth, torturing the bee
With madness, and unwonted reverie:
In Heaven, and all its environs, the leaf
And blossom of the fairy plant, in grief

Disconsolate linger—grief that hangs her head,
Repenting follies that full long have fled,
Heaving her white breast to the balmy air,
Like guilty beauty, chasten'd, and more fair:
Nyctanthes too, as sacred as the light
She fears to perfume, perfuming the night:
And Clytia pondering between many a sun,
While pettish tears adown her petals run:
And that aspiring flower that sprang on Earth—
And died, ere scarce exalted into birth,
Bursting its odorous heart in spirit to wing
Its way to Heaven, from garden of a king:
And Valisnerian lotus thither flown
From struggling with the waters of the Rhone:
And thy most lovely purple perfume, Zante!
Isola d'oro!—Fior di Levante!
And the Nelumbo bud that floats for ever
With Indian Cupid down the holy river—
Fair flowers, and fairy! to whose care is given
To bear the Goddess' song, in odors, up to Heaven:

> "Spirit! that dwellest where,
> In the deep sky,
> The terrible and fair,

In beauty vie!
Beyond the line of blue—
The boundary of the star
Which turneth at the view
Of thy barrier and thy bar—
Of the barrier overgone
By the comets who were cast
From their pride, and from their throne
To be drudges till the last—
To be carriers of fire
(The red fire of their heart)
With speed that may not tire
And with pain that shall not part—
Who livest—*that* we know—
In Eternity—we feel—
But the shadow of whose brow
What spirit shall reveal?
Tho' the beings whom thy Nesace,
Thy messenger hath known
Have dream'd for thy Infinity
A model of their own—
Thy will is done, Oh, God!
The star hath ridden high
Thro' many a tempest, but she rode

Beneath thy burning eye;
And here, in thought, to thee—
In thought that can alone
Ascend thy empire and so be
A partner of thy throne—
By winged Fantasy,
My embassy is given,
Till secrecy shall knowledge be
In the environs of Heaven."

She ceas'd—and buried then her burning cheek
Abash'd, amid the lilies there, to seek
A shelter from the fervor of His eye;
For the stars trembled at the Deity.
She stirr'd not—breath'd not—for a voice was there
How solemnly pervading the calm air!
A sound of silence on the startled ear
Which dreamy poets name "the music of the sphere."
Ours is a world of words: Quiet we call
"Silence"—which is the merest word of all.
All Nature speaks, and ev'n ideal things
Flap shadowy sounds from visionary wings—
But ah! not so when, thus, in realms on high
The eternal voice of God is passing by,
And the red winds are withering in the sky!

"What tho' in worlds which sightless cycles run,
Link'd to a little system, and one sun—
Where all my love is folly and the crowd
Still think my terrors but the thunder cloud,
The storm, the earthquake, and the ocean-wrath—
(Ah! will they cross me in my angrier path?)
What tho' in worlds which own a single sun
The sands of Time grow dimmer as they run,
Yet thine is my resplendency, so given
To bear my secrets thro' the upper Heaven.
Leave tenantless thy crystal home, and fly,
With all thy train, athwart the moony sky—
Apart—like fire-flies in Sicilian night,
And wing to other worlds another light!
Divulge the secrets of thy embassy
To the proud orbs that twinkle—and so be
To ev'ry heart a barrier and a ban
Lest the stars totter in the guilt of man!"

Up rose the maiden in the yellow night,
The single-mooned eve!—on Earth we plight
Our faith to one love—and one moon adore—
The birth-place of young Beauty had no more.
As sprang that yellow star from downy hours
Up rose the maiden from her shrine of flowers,
And bent o'er sheeny mountain and dim plain
Her way—but left not yet her Therasaean reign.

PART II

High on a mountain of enamell'd head—
Such as the drowsy shepherd on his bed
Of giant pasturage lying at his ease,
Raising his heavy eyelid, starts and sees
With many a mutter'd "hope to be forgiven"
What time the moon is quadrated in Heaven—
Of rosy head, that towering far away
Into the sunlit ether, caught the ray
Of sunken suns at eve—at noon of night,
While the moon danc'd with the fair stranger light—
Uprear'd upon such height arose a pile
Of gorgeous columns on th' unburthen'd air,
Flashing from Parian marble that twin smile
Far down upon the wave that sparkled there,
And nursled the young mountain in its lair.
Of molten stars their pavement, such as fall
Thro' the ebon air, besilvering the pall
Of their own dissolution, while they die—
Adorning then the dwellings of the sky.
A dome, by linked light from Heaven let down,
Sat gently on these columns as a crown—
A window of one circular diamond, there,
Look'd out above into the purple air,

And rays from God shot down that meteor chain
And hallow'd all the beauty twice again,
Save when, between th' Empyrean and that ring,
Some eager spirit flapp'd his dusky wing.
But on the pillars Seraph eyes have seen
The dimness of this world: that greyish green
That Nature loves the best for Beauty's grave
Lurk'd in each cornice, round each architrave—
And every sculptur'd cherub thereabout
That from his marble dwelling peeréd out
Seem'd earthly in the shadow of his niche—
Achaian statues in a world so rich?
Friezes from Tadmor and Persepolis—
From Balbec, and the stilly, clear abyss
Of beautiful Gomorrah! O, the wave
Is now upon thee—but too late to save!
Sound loves to revel in a summer night:
Witness the murmur of the grey twilight
That stole upon the ear, in Eyraco,
Of many a wild star-gazer long ago—
That stealeth ever on the ear of him
Who, musing, gazeth on the distance dim.
And sees the darkness coming as a cloud—
Is not its form—its voice—most palpable and loud?

But what is this?—it cometh—and it brings
A music with it—'tis the rush of wings—
A pause—and then a sweeping, falling strain
And Nesace is in her halls again.
From the wild energy of wanton haste
Her cheeks were flushing, and her lips apart;
And zone that clung around her gentle waist
Had burst beneath the heaving of her heart.
Within the center of that hall to breathe
She paus'd and panted, Zanthe! all beneath,
The fairy light that kiss'd her golden hair
And long'd to rest, yet could but sparkle there!
Young flowers were whispering in melody
To happy flowers that night—and tree to tree;
Fountains were gushing music as they fell
In many a star-lit grove, or moon-lit dell;
Yet silence came upon material things—
Fair flowers, bright waterfalls and angel wings—
And sound alone that from the spirit sprang
Bore burthen to the charm the maiden sang:

"'Neath blue-bell or streamer—
Or tufted wild spray
That keeps, from the dreamer,
The moonbeam away—
Bright beings! that ponder,
With half closing eyes,
On the stars which your wonder
Hath drawn from the skies,
Till they glance thro' the shade, and
Come down to your brow
Like—eyes of the maiden
Who calls on you now—
Arise! from your dreaming
In violet bowers,
To duty beseeming
These star-litten hours—
And shake from your tresses
Encumber'd with dew
The breath of those kisses
That cumber them too—
(O! how, without you, Love!
Could angels be blest?)
Those kisses of true love
That lull'd ye to rest!

Up!—shake from your wing
Each hindering thing:
The dew of the night—
It would weigh down your flight;
And true love caresses—
O! leave them apart!
They are light on the tresses,
But lead on the heart.
Ligeia! Ligeia!
My beautiful one!
Whose harshest idea
Will to melody run,
O! is it thy will
On the breezes to toss?
Or, capriciously still,
Like the lone Albatross,
Incumbent on night
(As she on the air)
To keep watch with delight
On the harmony there?

Ligeia! whatever
Thy image may be,
No magic shall sever

Thy music from thee.
Thou hast bound many eyes
In a dreamy sleep—
But the strains still arise
Which *thy* vigilance keep—
The sound of the rain
Which leaps down to the flower,
And dances again
In the rhythm of the shower—
The murmur that springs
From the growing of grass
Are the music of things—
But are modell'd, alas!—
Away, then my dearest,
O! hie thee away
To springs that lie clearest
Beneath the moon-ray—
To lone lake that smiles,
In its dream of deep rest,
At the many star-isles
That enjewel its breast—
Where wild flowers, creeping,
Have mingled their shade,
On its margin is sleeping

Full many a maid—
Some have left the cool glade, and
Have slept with the bee—
Arouse them my maiden,
On moorland and lea—
Go! breathe on their slumber,
All softly in ear,
The musical number
They slumber'd to hear—
For what can awaken
An angel so soon
Whose sleep hath been taken
Beneath the cold moon,
As the spell which no slumber
Of witchery may test,
The rythmical number
Which lull'd him to rest?"

Spirits in wing, and angels to the view,
A thousand seraphs burst th' Empyrean thro',
Young dreams still hovering on their drowsy flight—
Seraphs in all but "Knowledge," the keen light
That fell, refracted, thro' thy bounds, afar
O Death! from eye of God upon that star:

Sweet was that error—sweeter still that death—
Sweet was that error—ev'n with *us* the breath
Of science dims the mirror of our joy—
To them 't were the Simoom, and would destroy—
For what (to them) availeth it to know
That Truth is Falsehood—or that Bliss is Woe?
Sweet was their death—with them to die was rife
With the last ecstacy of satiate life—
Beyond that death no immortality—
But sleep that pondereth and is not "to be"—
And there—oh! may my weary spirit dwell—
Apart from Heaven's Eternity—and yet how far
from Hell!

What guilty spirit, in what shrubbery dim,
Heard not the stirring summons of that hymn?
But two: they fell: for Heaven no grace imparts
To those who hear not for their beating hearts.
A maiden-angel and her seraph-lover—
O! where (and ye may seek the wide skies over)
Was Love, the blind, near sober Duty known?
Unguided Love hath fallen—'mid "tears of
perfect moan."

He was a goodly spirit—he who fell:
A wanderer by moss-y-mantled well—
A gazer on the lights that shine above—
A dreamer in the moonbeam by his love:
What wonder? For each star is eye-like there,
And looks so sweetly down on Beauty's hair—
And they, and ev'ry mossy spring were holy
To his love-haunted heart and melancholy.
The night had found (to him a night of wo)
Upon a mountain crag, young Angelo—
Beetling it bends athwart the solemn sky,
And scowls on starry worlds that down beneath
it lie.
Here sate he with his love—his dark eye bent
With eagle gaze along the firmament:
Now turn'd it upon her—but ever then
It trembled to the orb of EARTH again.

"Iante, dearest, see! how dim that ray!
How lovely 'tis to look so far away!
She seem'd not thus upon that autumn eve
I left her gorgeous halls—nor mourn'd to leave.
That eve—that eve—I should remember well—
The sun-ray dropp'd, in Lemnos, with a spell

On th' Arabesque carving of a gilded hall
Wherein I sate, and on the draperied wall—
And on my eye-lids—O the heavy light!
How drowsily it weigh'd them into night!
On flowers, before, and mist, and love they ran
With Persian Saadi in his Gulistan:
But O that light!—I slumber'd—Death, the while,
Stole o'er my senses in that lovely isle
So softly that no single silken hair
Awoke that slept—or knew that it was there.
The last spot of Earth's orb I trod upon
Was a proud temple call'd the Parthenon—
More beauty clung around her column'd wall
Than ev'n thy glowing bosom beats withal,
And when old Time my wing did disenthral
Thence sprang I—as the eagle from his tower,
And years I left behind me in an hour.
What time upon her airy bounds I hung
One half the garden of her globe was flung
Unrolling as a chart unto my view—
Tenantless cities of the desert too!
Ianthe, beauty crowded on me then,
And half I wish'd to be again of men."

"My Angelo! and why of them to be?
A brighter dwelling-place is here for thee—
And greener fields than in yon world above,
And women's loveliness—and passionate love."
"But, list, Ianthe! when the air so soft
Fail'd, as my pennon'd spirit leapt aloft,
Perhaps my brain grew dizzy—but the world
I left so late .was into chaos hurl'd—
Sprang from her station, on the winds apart,
And roll'd, a flame, the fiery Heaven athwart.
Methought, my sweet one, then I ceased to soar
And fell—not swiftly as I rose before,
But with a downward, tremulous motion thro'
Light, brazen rays, this golden star unto!
Nor long the measure of my falling hours,
For nearest of all stars was thine to ours—
Dread star! that came, amid a night of mirth,
A red Daedalion on the timid Earth.

"We came—and to thy Earth—but not to us
Be given our lady's bidding to discuss:
We came, my love; around, above, below,
Gay fire-fly of the night we come and go,
Nor ask a reason save the angel-nod

She grants to us, as granted by her God—
But, Angelo, than thine grey Time unfurl'd
Never his fairy wing o'er fairier world!
Dim was its little disk, and angel eyes
Alone could see the phantom in the skies,
When first Al Aaraaf knew her course to be
Headlong thitherward o'er the starry sea—
But when its glory swell'd upon the sky,
As glowing Beauty's bust beneath man's eye,
We paus'd before the heritage of men,
And thy star trembled—as doth Beauty then!"

Thus, in discourse, the lovers whiled away
The night that waned and waned and brought no day.
They fell: for Heaven to them no hope imparts
Who hear not for the beating of their hearts.

40

SPIRITS OF THE DEAD

1

Thy soul shall find itself alone
'Mid dark thoughts of the grey tomb-stone—
Not one, of all the crowd, to pry
Into thine hour of secrecy:

2

Be silent in that solitude
Which is not loneliness—for then
The spirits of the dead who stood
In life before thee are again
In death around thee—and their will
Shall then overshadow thee: be still.

3

For the night—tho' clear—shall frown—
And the stars shall look not down,
From their high thrones in the Heaven,

With light like Hope to mortals given—
But their red orbs, without beam,
To thy weariness shall seem
As a burning and a fever
Which would cling to thee for ever:

4

Now are thoughts thou shalt not banish—
Now are visions ne'er to vanish—
From thy spirit shall they pass
No more—like dew-drop from the grass:

5

The breeze—the breath of God—is still—
And the mist upon the hill
Shadowy—shadowy—yet unbroken,
Is a symbol and a token—
How it hangs upon the trees,
A mystery of mysteries!—

HENRY WADSWORTH LONGFELLOW

1807–1882

41

A PSALM OF LIFE

What the Heart of the Young Man
Said to the Psalmist.

Tell me not, in mournful numbers,
Life is but an empty dream![7]
For the soul is dead that slumbers,
And things are not what they seem.

Life is real! Life is earnest!
And the grave is not its goal;
Dust thou art, to dust returnest,
Was not spoken of the soul.

---

7   Eric S Robertson in The Life of Henry Wadsworth
Longfellow wrote that this poem 'proclaims the gladness
of living to be the best of poetry. It is not the best of
poetry, but it makes the best theme for a preacher.' He also
mentions that the poem was being talked about amongst
the preachers and sung as a hymn in churches.

Not enjoyment, and not sorrow,
Is our destined end or way;
But to act, that each to-morrow
Find us farther than to-day.

Art is long, and Time is fleeting,
And our hearts, though stout and brave,
Still, like muffled drums, are beating
Funeral marches to the grave.

In the world's broad field of battle,
In the bivouac of Life,
Be not like dumb, driven cattle!
Be a hero in the strife!

Trust no Future, howe'er pleasant!
Let the dead Past bury its dead!
Act,— act in the living Present!
Heart within, and God o'erhead!

Lives of great men all remind us
We can make our lives sublime,
And, departing, leave behind us
Footprints on the sands of time;

Footprints, that perhaps another,
Sailing o'er life's solemn main,
A forlorn and shipwrecked brother,
Seeing, shall take heart again.

Let us, then, be up and doing,
With a heart for any fate;
Still achieving, still pursuing,
Learn to labor and to wait.

42

THE DAY IS DONE

The day is done, and the darkness
Falls from the wings of Night,
As a feather is wafted downward
From an eagle in his flight.

I see the lights of the village
Gleam through the rain and the mist,
And a feeling of sadness comes o'er me
That my soul cannot resist:

A feeling of sadness and longing,
That is not akin to pain,
And resembles sorrow only
As the mist resembles the rain.

Come, read to me some poem,
Some simple and heartfelt lay,
That shall soothe this restless feeling,
And banish the thoughts of day.

Not from the grand old masters,
Not from the bards sublime,
Whose distant footsteps echo
Through the corridors of Time.

For, like strains of martial music,
Their mighty thoughts suggest
Life's endless toil and endeavor;
And to-night I long for rest.

Read from some humbler poet,
Whose songs gushed from his heart,
As showers from the clouds of summer,
Or tears from the eyelids start;

Who, through long days of labor,
And nights devoid of ease,
Still heard in his soul the music
Of wonderful melodies.

Such songs have power to quiet
The restless pulse of care,
And come like the benediction
That follows after prayer.

Then read from the treasured volume
The poem of thy choice,
And lend to the rhyme of the poet
The beauty of thy voice.

And the night shall be filled with music,
And the cares, that infest the day,
Shall fold their tents, like the Arabs,
And as silently steal away.

43

EXCELSIOR

The shades of night were falling fast,
As through an Alpine village passed
A youth, who bore, 'mid snow and ice,
A banner with the strange device,
    Excelsior!

His brow was sad; his eye beneath,
Flashed like a falchion from its sheath,
And like a silver clarion rung
The accents of that unknown tongue,
    Excelsior!

In happy homes he saw the light
Of household fires gleam warm and bright;
Above, the spectral glaciers shone,
And from his lips escaped a groan,
    Excelsior!

"Try not the Pass!" the old man said:
"Dark lowers the tempest overhead,
The roaring torrent is deep and wide!
And loud that clarion voice replied,
　　Excelsior!

"Oh stay," the maiden said, "and rest
Thy weary head upon this breast!"
A tear stood in his bright blue eye,
But still he answered, with a sigh,
　　Excelsior!

"Beware the pine-tree's withered branch!
Beware the awful avalanche!"
This was the peasant's last Good-night,
A voice replied, far up the height,
　　Excelsior!

At break of day, as heavenward
The pious monks of Saint Bernard
Uttered the oft-repeated prayer,
A voice cried through the startled air,
　　Excelsior!

A traveller, by the faithful hound,
Half-buried in the snow was found,
Still grasping in his hand of ice
That banner with the strange device,
    Excelsior!

There in the twilight cold and gray,
Lifeless, but beautiful, he lay,
And from the sky, serene and far,
A voice fell, like a falling star,
    Excelsior!

44

THE SLAVE'S DREAM

Beside the ungathered rice he lay,
His sickle in his hand;
His breast was bare, his matted hair
Was buried in the sand.
Again, in the mist and shadow of sleep,
He saw his Native Land.

Wide through the landscape of his dreams
The lordly Niger flowed;
Beneath the palm-trees on the plain
Once more a king he strode;
And heard the tinkling caravans
Descend the mountain-road.

He saw once more his dark-eyed queen
Among her children stand;
They clasped his neck, they kissed his cheeks,

They held him by the hand!—
A tear burst from the sleeper's lids
And fell into the sand.

And then at furious speed he rode
Along the Niger's bank;
His bridle-reins were golden chains,
And, with a martial clank,
At each leap he could feel his scabbard of steel
Smiting his stallion's flank.

Before him, like a blood-red flag,
The bright flamingoes flew;
From morn till night he followed their flight,
O'er plains where the tamarind grew,
Till he saw the roofs of Caffre huts,
And the ocean rose to view.

At night he heard the lion roar,
And the hyena scream,
And the river-horse, as he crushed the reeds
Beside some hidden stream;
And it passed, like a glorious roll of drums,
Through the triumph of his dream.

The forests, with their myriad tongues,
Shouted of liberty;
And the Blast of the Desert cried aloud,
With a voice so wild and free,
That he started in his sleep and smiled
At their tempestuous glee.

He did not feel the driver's whip,
Nor the burning heat of day;
For Death had illumined the Land of Sleep,
And his lifeless body lay
A worn-out fetter, that the soul
Had broken and thrown away!

RALPH WALDO EMERSON

1803-1882

45

BRAHMA

If the red slayer think he slays,
Or if the slain think he is slain,
They know not well the subtle ways
I keep, and pass, and turn again.

Far or forgot to me is near;
Shadow and sunlight are the same;
The vanished gods to me appear;
And one to me are shame and fame.

They reckon ill who leave me out;
When me they fly, I am the wings;
I am the doubter and the doubt,
I am the hymn the Brahmin sings.

The strong gods pine for my abode,
And pine in vain the sacred Seven;
But thou, meek lover of the good!
Find me, and turn thy back on heaven.

46

BOSTON HYMN

The word of the Lord by night
To the watching Pilgrims came,
As they sat by the seaside,
And filled their hearts with flame.

God said, I am tired of kings,
I suffer them no more;
Up to my ear the morning brings
The outrage of the poor.

Think ye I made this ball
A field of havoc and war,
Where tyrants great and tyrants small
Might harry the weak and poor?

My angel, his name is Freedom,—
Choose him to be your king;
He shall cut pathways east and west,
And fend you with his wing.

Lo! I uncover the land
Which I hid of old time in the West,
As the sculptor uncovers the statue
When he has wrought his best;

I show Columbia, of the rocks
Which dip their foot in the seas,
And soar to the air-borne flocks
Of clouds, and the boreal fleece.

I will divide my goods;
Call in the wretch and slave:
None shall rule but the humble,
And none but Toil shall have.

I will have never a noble,
No lineage counted great;
Fishers and choppers and ploughmen
Shall constitute a state.

Go, cut down trees in the forest,
And trim the straightest boughs;
Cut down the trees in the forest,
And build me a wooden house.

Call the people together,
The young men and the sires,

The digger in the harvest field,
Hireling, and him that hires;

And here in a pine state-house
They shall choose men to rule
In every needful faculty,
In church, and state, and school.

Lo, now! if these poor men
Can govern the land and sea,
And make just laws below the sun,
As planets faithful be.

And ye shall succour men;
'T is nobleness to serve;
Help them who cannot help again:
Beware from right to swerve.

I break your bonds and masterships,
And I unchain the slave:
Free be his heart and hand henceforth
As wind and wandering wave.

I cause from every creature
His proper good to flow:

As much as he is and doeth,
So much he shall bestow.

But laying hands on another
To coin his labour and sweat,
He goes in pawn to his victim
For eternal years in debt.

To-day unbind the captive,
So only are ye unbound;
Lift up a people from the dust,
Trump of their rescue, sound!

Pay ransom to the owner,
And fill the bag to the brim.
Who is the owner? The slave is owner,
And ever was. Pay him.

O North! give him beauty for rags,
And honour, O South! for his shame;
Nevada! coin thy golden crags
With Freedom's image and name.

Up! and the dusky race
That sat in darkness long,—

Be swift their feet as antelopes,
And as behemoth strong.

Come, East and West and North,
By races, as snow-flakes,
And carry my purpose forth,
Which neither halts nor shakes.

My will fulfilled shall be,
For, in daylight or in dark,
My thunderbolt has eyes to see
His way home to the mark.

HENRY DAVID THOREAU

1817–1862

47

THE SUMMER RAIN

My books I'd fain cast off, I cannot read,
'Twixt every page my thoughts go stray at large
Down in the meadow, where is richer feed,
And will not mind to hit their proper targe.

Plutarch was good, and so was Homer too,
Our Shakespeare's life were rich to live again,
What Plutarch read, that was not good nor true,
Nor Shakespeare's books, unless his books were men.

Here while I lie beneath this walnut bough,
What care I for the Greeks or for Troy town,
If juster battles are enacted now
Between the ants upon this hummock's crown?

Bid Homer wait till I the issue learn,
If red or black the gods will favor most,
Or yonder Ajax will the phalanx turn,
Struggling to heave some rock against the host.

Tell Shakespeare to attend some leisure hour,
For now I've business with this drop of dew,
And see you not, the clouds prepare a shower—
I'll meet him shortly when the sky is blue.

This bed of herd's grass and wild oats was spread
Last year with nicer skill than monarchs use.
A clover tuft is pillow for my head,
And violets quite overtop my shoes.

And now the cordial clouds have shut all in,
And gently swells the wind to say all's well;
The scattered drops are falling fast and thin,
Some in the pool, some in the flower-bell.

I am well drenched upon my bed of oats;
But see that globe come rolling down its stem,
Now like a lonely planet there it floats,
And now it sinks into my garment's hem.

Drip drip the trees for all the country round,
And richness rare distills from every bough;
The wind alone it is makes every sound,
Shaking down crystals on the leaves below.

For shame the sun will never show himself,
Who could not with his beams e'er melt me so;
My dripping locks—they would become an elf,
Who in a beaded coat does gayly go.

48

INSPIRATION

Whate'er we leave to God, God does,
And blesses us;
The work we choose should be our own,
God leaves alone.

If with light head erect I sing,
Though all the Muses lend their force,
From my poor love of anything,
The verse is weak and shallow as its source.

But if with bended neck I grope
Listening behind me for my wit,
With faith superior to hope,
More anxious to keep back than forward it;

Making my soul accomplice there
Unto the flame my heart hath lit,
Then will the verse for ever wear—
Time cannot bend the line which God hath writ.

Always the general show of things
Floats in review before my mind,
And such true love and reverence brings,
That sometimes I forget that I am blind.

But now there comes unsought, unseen,
Some clear divine electuary,
And I, who had but sensual been,
Grow sensible, and as God is, am wary.

I hearing get, who had but ears,
And sight, who had but eyes before,
I moments live, who lived but years,
And truth discern, who knew but learning's lore.

I hear beyond the range of sound,
I see beyond the range of sight,
New earths and skies and seas around,
And in my day the sun doth pale his light.

A clear and ancient harmony
Pierces my soul through all its din,
As through its utmost melody,—
Farther behind than they, farther within.

More swift its bolt than lightning is,
Its voice than thunder is more loud,
It doth expand my privacies
To all, and leave me single in the crowd.

It speaks with such authority,
With so serene and lofty tone,
That idle Time runs gadding by,
And leaves me with Eternity alone.

Now chiefly is my natal hour,
And only now my prime of life,
Of manhood's strength it is the flower,
'Tis peace's end and war's beginning strife.

It comes in summer's broadest noon,
By a grey wall or some chance place,
Unseasoning Time, insulting June,
And vexing day with its presuming face.

Such fragrance round my couch it makes,
More rich than are Arabian drugs,
That my soul scents its life and wakes
The body up beneath its perfumed rugs.

Such is the Muse, the heavenly maid,
The star that guides our mortal course,
Which shows where life's true kernel's laid,
Its wheat's fine flour, and its undying force.

She with one breath attunes the spheres,
And also my poor human heart,
With one impulse propels the years
Around, and gives my throbbing pulse its start.

I will not doubt for evermore,
Nor falter from a steadfast faith,
For though the system be turned o'er,
God takes not back the word which once he saith.

I will not doubt the love untold
Which not my worth nor want has bought,
Which wooed me young, and wooes me old,
And to this evening hath me brought.

My memory I'll educate
To know the one historic truth,
Remembering to the latest date
The only true and sole immortal youth.

Be but thy inspiration given,
No matter through what danger sought,
I'll fathom hell or climb to heaven,
And yet esteem that cheap which love has bought.

Fame cannot tempt the bard
Who's famous with his God,
Nor laurel him reward
Who has his Maker's nod.

49

FRIENDSHIP

'Friends, Romans, Countrymen, and Lovers.'

Let such pure hate still underprop
Our love, that we may be
Each other's conscience,
And have our sympathy
Mainly from thence.

We'll one another treat like gods,
And all the faith we have
In virtue and in truth, bestow
On either, and suspicion leave
To gods below.

Two solitary stars—
Unmeasured systems far
Between us roll;
But by our conscious light we are
Determined to one pole.

What need confound the sphere?—
Love can afford to wait;
For it no hour's too late
That witnesseth one duty's end,
Or to another doth beginning lend.

It will subserve no use,
More than the tints of flowers;
Only the independent guest
Frequents its bowers,
Inherits its bequest.

No speech, though kind, has it;
But kinder silence doles
Unto its mates;
By night consoles,
By day congratulates.

What saith the tongue to tongue?
What heareth ear of ear?
By the decrees of fate
From year to year,
Does it communicate.

Pathless the gulf of feeling yawns;
No trivial bridge of words,
Or arch of boldest span,
Can leap the moat that girds
The sincere man.

No show of bolts and bars
Can keep the foeman out,
Or 'scape his secret mine,
Who entered with the doubt
That drew the line.

No warder at the gate
Can let the friendly in;
But, like the sun, o'er all
He will the castle win,
And shine along the wall.

There's nothing in the world I know
That can escape from love,
For every depth it goes below,
And every height above.

It waits, as waits the sky
Until the clouds go by,
Yet shines serenely on
With an eternal day,
Alike when they are gone,
And when they stay.

Implacable is Love,—
Foes may be bought or teased
From their hostile intent,
But he goes unappeased
Who is on kindness bent.

50

HAZE

Woof of the sun, ethereal gauze,
Woven of Nature's richest stuffs,
Visible heat, air-water, and dry sea,
Last conquest of the eye;
Toil of the day displayed, sun-dust,
Aerial surf upon the shores of earth,
Ethereal estuary, frith of light,
Breakers of air, billows of heat,
Fine summer spray on inland seas;
Bird of the sun, transparent-winged,
Owlet of noon, soft-pinioned,
From heath or stubble rising without song,—
Establish thy serenity o'er the fields.

51

SMOKE

Light-winged Smoke, Icarian bird,
Melting thy pinions in thy upward flight;
Lark without song, and messenger of dawn,
Circling above the hamlets as thy nest;
Or else, departing dream, and shadowy form
Of midnight vision, gathering up thy skirts;
By night star-veiling, and by day
Darkening the light and blotting out the sun;
Go thou, my incense, upward from this hearth,
And ask the gods to pardon this clear flame.

52

THE FUNERAL BELL

One more is gone
Out of the busy throng
That tread these paths;
The church-bell tolls,
Its sad knell rolls
To many hearths.

Flower-bells toll not,
Their echoes roll not
Upon my ear;
There still perchance
That gentle spirit haunts
A fragrant bier.

Low lies the pall,
Lowly the mourners all

Their passage grope;
No sable hue
Mars the serene blue
Of heaven's cope.

In distant dell
Faint sounds the funeral bell;
A heavenly chime;
Some poet there
Weaves the light-burthened air
Into sweet rhyme.

53

NATURE

O Nature! I do not aspire
To be the highest in thy quire,—
To be a meteor in the sky,
Or comet that may range on high;
Only a zephyr that may blow
Among the reeds by the river low;
Give me thy most privy place
Where to run my airy race.

In some withdrawn, unpublic mead
Let me sigh upon a reed,
Or in the woods, with leafy din,
Whisper the still evening in:
Some still work give me to do,—
Only—be it near to you!

For I'd rather be thy child
And pupil, in the forest wild,
Than be the king of men elsewhere,
And most sovereign slave of care:
To have one moment of thy dawn,
Than share the city's year forlorn.

54

THE MOON

'Time wears her not; she doth his chariot guide;
Mortality below her orb is placed.'—RALEIGH.

The full-orbed moon with unchanged ray
Mounts up the eastern sky,
Not doomed to these short nights for aye,
But shining steadily.

She does not wane, but my fortùne,
Which her rays do not bless;
My wayward path declineth soon,
But she shines not the less.

And if she faintly glimmers here
And palèd is her light,
Yet always in her proper sphere
She's mistress of the night.

ANNE
BRADSTREET

1612-1672

55

CONTEMPLATIONS

Some time now past in the Autumnal Tide,
When Phoebus wanted but one hour to bed,
The trees all richly clad, yet void of pride
Were gilded o'er by his rich golden head.
Their leaves and fruits, seem'd painted, but
was true
Of green, of red, of yellow, mixed hue,
Rapt were my senses at this delectable view.

I wist not what to wish, yet sure, thought I,
If so much excellence abide below,
How excellent is He that dwells on high!
Whose power and beauty by his works we
know;
Sure he is goodness, wisdom, glory, light,
That hath this underworld so richly dight:
More Heaven than Earth was here, no winter
and no night.

Then on a stately oak I cast mine eye,
Whose ruffling top the clouds seem'd to aspire;
How long since thou wast in thine infancy?
Thy strength, and stature, more thy years admire;
Hath hundred winters past since thou wast born,
Or thousand since thou breakest thy shell
of horn?
If so, all these as naught Eternity doth scorn.

I heard the merry grasshopper then sing,
The black-clad cricket bear a second part,
They kept one tune, and played on the same
string,
Seeming to glory in their little art.
Shall creatures abject thus their voices raise?
And in their kind resound their Master's praise:
Whilst I, as mute, can warble forth no higher lays.

When I behold the heavens as in their prime,
And then the earth (though old) still clad in
green,
The stones and trees, insensible of time,
Nor age nor wrinkle on their front are seen;
If winter come, and greenness then do fade,
A spring returns, and they more youthful made;
But Man grows old, lies down, remains where
once he's laid.

56

THE DAY OF DOOM

SOUNDING OF THE LAST TRUMP

Still was the night, Serene & Bright,
when all Men sleeping lay;
Calm was the season, & carnal reason
thought so 'twould last for ay.
Soul, take thine ease, let sorrow cease,
much good thou hast in store:
This was their Song, thei   r Cups
among,
the Evening before.

Wallowing in all kind of sin,
vile wretches lay secure:
The best of men had scarcely then
their Lamps kept in good ure.
Virgins unwise, who through disguise
amongst the best were number'd,
Had closed their eyes; yea, and the wise
through sloth and frailty slumber'd.

For at midnight brake forth a Light,
which turn'd the night to day,
And speedily a hideous cry
did all the world dismay.
Sinners awake, their hearts do ake,
trembling their loynes surprizeth;
Amaz'd with fear, by what they hear,
each one of them ariseth.

They rush from Beds with giddy heads,
and to their windows run,
Viewing this light, which shines more bright
than doth the Noon-day Sun.
Straightway appears (they see 't with tears)
the Son of God most dread;
Who with his Train comes on amain
to Judge both Quick and Dead.

Before his face the Heav'ns gave place,
and Skies are rent asunder,
With mighty voice, and hideous noise,
more terrible than Thunder.
His brightness damps heav'ns glorious lamps

and makes them hang their heads,
As if afraid and quite dismay'd,
they quit their wonted steads.

No heart so bold, but now grows cold
and almost dead with fear:
No eye so dry, but now can cry,
and pour out many a tear.
Earth's Potentates and pow'rful States,
Captains and Men of Might
Are quite abasht, their courage dasht
at this most dreadful sight.

Mean men lament, great men do rent
their Robes, and tear their hair:
They do not spare their flesh to tear
through horrible despair.
All Kindreds wail: all hearts do fail:
horror the world doth fill
With weeping eyes, and loud out-cries,
yet knows not how to kill.

Some hide themselves in Caves and Delves,
in places under ground:

Some rashly leap into the Deep,
to scape by being drown'd:
Some to the Rocks (O senseless blocks!)
and woody Mountains run,
That there they might this fearful sight,
and dreaded Presence shun.

In vain do they to Mountains say,
fall on us and us hide
From Judges ire, more hot than fire,
for who may it abide?
No hiding place can from his Face
sinners at all conceal,
Whose flaming Eye hid things doth 'spy
and darkest things reveal.

The Judge draws nigh, exalted high,
upon a lofty Throne,
Amidst a throng of Angels strong,
lo, Israel's Holy One!
The excellence of whose presence
and awful Majesty,
Amazeth Nature, and every Creature,
doth more than terrify.

The Mountains smoak, the Hills are shook,
the Earth is rent and torn,
As if she should be clear dissolv'd,
or from the Center born.
The Sea doth roar, forsakes the shore,
and shrinks away for fear;
The wild beasts flee into the Sea,
so soon as he draws near.

Before his Throne a Trump is blown,
Proclaiming the day of Doom:
Forthwith he cries, Ye dead arise,
and unto Judgment come.
No sooner said, but 'tis obey'd;
Sepulchres opened are:
Dead bodies all rise at his call,
and 's mighty power declare.

His winged Hosts flie through all Coasts,
together gathering
Both good and bad, both quick and dead,
and all to Judgment bring.
Out of their holes those creeping Moles,

that hid themselves for fear,
By force they take, and quickly make
before the Judge appear.

Thus every one before the Throne
of Christ the Judge is brought,
Both righteous and impious
that good or ill hath wrought.
A separation, and diff'ring station
by Christ appointed is
(To sinners sad) 'twixt good and bad,
'twixt Heirs of woe and bliss.

JOHN GREENLEAF WHITTIER

1807–1892

57

SKIPPER IRESON'S RIDE

Of all the rides since the birth of time,
Told in story or sung in rhyme,—
On Apuleius's Golden Ass,
Or one-eyed Calendar's horse of brass,
Witch astride of a human back,
Islam's prophet on Al-Borak,—
The strangest ride that ever was sped
Was Ireson's, out from Marblehead!
Old Floyd Ireson, for his hard heart,
Tarred and feathered and carried in a cart
By the women of Marblehead!

Body of turkey, head of owl,
Wings a-droop like a rained-on fowl,
Feathered and ruffled in every part,
Skipper Ireson stood in the cart.
Scores of women, old and young,
Strong of muscle, and glib of tongue,

Pushed and pulled up the rocky lane,
Shouting and singing the shrill refrain
"Here's Flud Oirson, for his horrd horrt,
Torr'd an' futherr'd an' corr'd in a corrt
By the women o' Morble'ead!"

Wrinkled scolds with hands on hips,
Girls in bloom of cheek and lips,
Wild-eyed, free-limbed, such as chase
Bacchus round some antique vase,
Brief of skirt, with ankles bare,
Loose of kerchief and loose of hair,

With conch-shells blowing and fish-horns' twang.
Over and over the Maenads sang:
"Here's Flud Oirson, fur his horrd horrt,
Torr'd an' futherr'd an' corr'd in a corrt
By the women o' Morble'ead!"

Small pity for him!—He sailed away
From a leaking ship, in Chaleur Bay,—
Sailed away from a sinking wreck,
With his own town's-people on her deck!
"Lay by! lay by!" they called to him.

Back he answered, "Sink or swim!
Brag of your catch of fish again!"
And off he sailed through the fog and rain!
Old Floyd Ireson, for his hard heart,
Tarred and feathered and carried in a cart
By the women of Marblehead!

Fathoms deep in dark Chaleur
That wreck shall lie forevermore.
Mother and sister, wife and maid,
Looked from the rocks of Marblehead
Over the moaning and rainy sea,—
Looked for the coming that might not be!
What did the winds and the sea-birds say
Of the cruel captain who sailed away?—
Old Floyd Ireson, for his hard heart,
Tarred and feathered and carried in a cart
By the women of Marblehead!

Through the street, on either side,
Up flew windows, doors swung wide;

Sharp-tongued spinsters, old wives gray,
Treble lent the fish-horn's bray.

Sea-worn grandsires, cripple-bound,
Hulks of old sailors run aground,
Shook head, and fist, and hat, and cane,
And cracked with curses the old refrain:
"Here's Flud Oirson, fur his horrd horrt,
Torr'd an' futherr'd an' corr'd in a corrt
By the women o' Morble'ead!

Sweetly along the Salem road
Bloom of orchard and lilac showed.
Little the wicked skipper knew
Of the fields so green and the sky so blue.
Riding there in his sorry trim,
Like an Indian idol glum and grim,
Scarcely he seemed the sound to hear
Of voices shouting, far and near:
"Here's Flud Oirson, fur his horrd horrt,
Torr'd an' futherr'd an' corr'd in a corrt
By the women o' Morble'ead!"

"Hear me, neighbors!" at last he cried,"—
What to me is this noisy ride?
What is the shame that clothes the skin
To the nameless horror that lives within?

Waking or sleeping, I see a wreck,
And hear a cry from a reeling deck!
Hate me and curse me,—I only dread
The hand of God and the face of the dead!"
Said old Floyd Ireson, for his hard heart,
Tarred and feathered and carried in a cart
By the women of Marblehead!

Then the wife of the skipper lost at sea
Said, God has touched him! why should we?"
Said an old wife mourning her only son,
"Cut the rogue's tether and let him run!"
So with soft relentings and rude excuse,
Half scorn, half pity, they cut him loose,
And gave him a cloak to hide him in,
And left him alone with his shame and sin.
Poor Floyd Ireson, for his hard heart,
Tarred and feathered and carried in a cart
By the women of Marblehead!

58

MAUD MULLER

Maud Muller, on a summer's day,
Raked the meadow sweet with hay.

Beneath her torn hat glowed the wealth
Of simple beauty and rustic health.

Singing, she wrought, and her merry glee
The mock-bird echoed from his tree.

But when she glanced to the far-off town,
White from its hill-slope looking down,

The sweet song died, and a vague unrest
And a nameless longing filled her breast,

A wish, that she hardly dared to own,
For something better than she had known.

The Judge rode slowly down the lane,
Smoothing his horse's chestnut mane.

He drew his bridle in the shade
Of the apple-trees, to greet the maid,

And ask a draught from the spring that flowed
Through the meadow across the road.

She stooped where the cool spring bubbled up,
And filled for him her small tin cup,

And blushed as she gave it, looking down
On her feet so bare, and her tattered gown.

"Thanks!" said the Judge; "a sweeter draught
From a fairer hand was never quaffed."

He spoke of the grass and flowers and trees,
Of the singing birds and the humming bees;

Then talked of the haying, and wondered whether
The cloud in the west would bring foul weather.

And Maud forgot her brier-torn gown,
And her graceful ankles bare and brown;

And listened, while a pleased surprise
Looked from her long-lashed hazel eyes.

At last, like one who for delay
Seeks a vain excuse, he rode away.

Maud Muller looked and sighed: "Ah me!
That I the Judge's bride might be!

"He would dress me up in silks so fine,
And praise and toast me at his wine.

"My father should wear a broadcloth coat;
My brother should sail a painted boat.

"I'd dress my mother so grand and gay,
And the baby should have a new toy each day.

"And I'd feed the hungry and clothe the poor
And all should bless me who left our door."

The Judge looked back as he climbed the hill,
And saw Maud Muller standing still.

"A form more fair, a face more sweet
Ne'er hath it been my lot to meet.

"And her modest answer and graceful air
Show her wise and good as she is fair.

"Would she were mine, and I to-day,
Like her, a harvester of hay

"No doubtful balance of rights and wrongs,
Nor weary lawyers with endless tongues,

"But low of cattle and song of birds,
And health and quiet and loving words."

But he thought of his sisters, proud and cold,
And his mother, vain of her rank and gold.

So, closing his heart, the Judge rode on,
And Maud was left in the field alone.

But the lawyers smiled that afternoon,
When he hummed in court an old love-tune;

And the young girl mused beside the well,
Till the rain on the unraked clover,

He wedded a wife of richest dower,
Who lived for fashion, as he for power.

Yet oft, in his marble hearth's bright glow,
He watched a picture come and go;

And sweet Maud Muller's hazel eyes
Looked out in their innocent surprise.

Oft, when the wine in his glass was red,
He longed for the wayside well instead;

And closed his eyes on his garnished rooms
To dream of meadows and clover-blooms.

And the proud man sighed, with a secret pain,
"Ah, that I were free again!

"Free as when I rode that day,
Where the barefoot maiden raked her hay."

She wedded a man unlearned and poor,
And many children played round her door.

But care and sorrow, and childbirth pain,
Left their traces on heart and brain.

And oft, when the summer sun shone hot
On the new-mown hay in the meadow lot,

And she heard the little spring brook fall
Over the roadside, through the wall;

In the shade of the apple-tree again
She saw a rider draw his rein.

And gazing down with timid grace
She felt his pleased eyes read her face.

Sometimes her narrow kitchen walls
Stretched away into stately halls;

The weary wheel to a spinnet turned,
The tallow candle an astral burned,

And for him who sat by the chimney lug,
Dozing and grumbling o'er pipe and mug,

A manly form at her side she saw,
And joy was duty and love was law.

Then she took up her burden of life again,
Saying only, "it might have been."

Alas for maiden, alas for Judge,
For rich repiner and household drudge!

God pity them both! and pity us all,
Who vainly the dreams of youth recall.

For of all sad words of tongue or pen,
The saddest are these: "It might have been!"

Ah, well! for us all some sweet hope lies
Deeply buried from human eyes;

And, in the hereafter, angels may
Roll the stone from its grave away!

THOMAS BUCHANAN READ

(1822–1872)

59

STORM ON ST. BERNARD

Oh, Heaven, it is a fearful thing
Beneath the tempest's beating wing
To struggle, like a stricken hare
When swoops the monarch bird of air;
To breast the loud winds' fitful spasms,
To brave the cloud and shun the chasms,
Tossed like a fretted shallop-sail
Between the ocean and the gale.

Along the valley, loud and fleet,
The rising tempest leapt and roared,
And scaled the Alp, till from his seat
The throned Eternity of Snow
His frequent avalanches poured
In thunder to the storm below.

And now, to crown their fears, a roar
Like ocean battling with the shore,

Or like that sound which night and day
Breaks through Niagara's veil of spray,
From some great height within the cloud,

To some unmeasured valley driven,
Swept down, and with a voice so loud
It seemed as it would shatter heaven!
The bravest quailed; it swept so near,
It made the ruddiest cheek to blanch,
While look replied to look in fear,
"The avalanche! The avalanche!"
It forced the foremost to recoil,
Before its sideward billows thrown,—
Who cried, "O God! Here ends our toil!
The path is overswept and gone!"

The night came down. The ghostly dark,
Made ghostlier by its sheet of snow,
Wailed round them its tempestuous wo,
Like Death's announcing courier! "Hark
There, heard you not the alp-hound's bark?
And there again! and there! Ah, no,
'Tis but the blast that mocks us so!"

Then through the thick and blackening mist
Death glared on them, and breathed so near,
Some felt his breath grow almost warm,
The while he whispered in their ear
Of sleep that should out-dream the storm.
Then lower drooped their lids,—when, "List!
Now, heard you not the storm-bell ring?
And there again, and twice and thrice!
Ah, no, 'tis but the thundering
Of tempests on a crag of ice!"

Death smiled on them, and it seemed good
On such a mellow bed to lie
The storm was like a lullaby,
And drowsy pleasure soothed their blood.
But still the sturdy, practised guide
His unremitting labour plied;
Now this one shook until he woke,
And closer wrapt the other's cloak,—
Still shouting with his utmost breath,
To startle back the hand of Death,
Brave words of cheer! "But, hark again,—
Between the blasts the sound is plain;
The storm, inhaling, lulls,—and hark!

It is—it is! the alp-dog's bark
And on the tempest's passing swell—
The voice of cheer so long debarred—
There swings the Convent's guiding-bell,
The sacred bell of Saint Bernard!"

60

DRIFTING

My soul to-day
Is far away,
Sailing the Vesuvian Bay;
My winged boat
A bird afloat,
Swings round the purple peaks
remote:—

Round purple peaks
It sails, and seeks
Blue inlets and their crystal creeks,
Where high rocks throw,
Through deeps below,
A duplicated golden glow.

Far, vague, and dim,
The mountains swim;

While an Vesuvius' misty brim,
With outstretched hands,
The gray smoke stands
O'erlooking the volcanic lands.

Here Ischia smiles
O'er liquid miles;
And yonder, bluest of the isles,
Calm Capri waits,
Her sapphire gates
Beguiling to her bright estates.

I heed not, if
My rippling skiff
Float swift or slow from cliff to cliff;
With dreamful eyes
My spirit lies
Under the walls of Paradise.

Under the walls
Where swells and falls
The Bay's deep breast at intervals
At peace I lie,
Blown softly by,
A cloud upon this liquid sky.

The day, so mild,
Is Heaven's own child,
With Earth and Ocean reconciled;
The airs I feel
Around me steal
Are murmuring to the murmuring keel.

Over the rail
My hand I trail
Within the shadow of the sail,
A joy intense,
The cooling sense
Glides down my drowsy indolence.

With dreamful eyes
My spirit lies
Where Summer sings and never dies,
O'erveiled with vines
She glows and shines
Among her future oil and wines.

Her children, hid
The cliffs amid,
Are gambolling with the gambolling kid;
Or down the walls,

With tipsy calls,
Laugh on the rocks like waterfalls.

The fisher's child,
With tresses wild,
Unto the smooth, bright sand beguiled,
With glowing lips
Sings as she skips,
Or gazes at the far-off ships.

Yon deep bark goes
Where traffic blows,
From lands of sun to lands of snows;
This happier one,—
Its course is run
From lands of snow to lands of sun.

O happy ship,
To rise and dip,
With the blue crystal at your lip!
O happy crew,
My heart with you
Sails, and sails, and sings anew!

No more, no more
The worldly shore
Upbraids me with its loud uproar
With dreamful eyes
My spirit lies
Under the walls of Paradise!